To Alfred, whose hand is in the box.

nonagon
books

The American Centrist: A Moderate Manifesto

Copyright © 2025, Brent Jones.

All rights reserved.

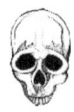

"You know," said Elias, forgetting about his injuries for a moment as his naturally inquisitive nature got the better of him, "the same picture can be applied to many things." He put his palms together. "Centrist and utilitarian." He then started to separate his hands tracing out a circle, saying, "Liberal and conservative. Socialist and populist. Communist and fascist, and there we are at the back side of the circle. From an orthogonal viewpoint, the spectrum really runs from democratic to autocratic. The *left* and the *right* are just different paths to the same unfortunate end." He slumped as his exhaustion started to take hold. "I'm sorry to say that humanity will see this one again in another twenty years or so…with a vengeance." His voice trailed off at the end as it seemed that he had suddenly remembered that he had been hit over the head multiple times by an eldritch monster, probably had a concussion, and thus fell promptly unconscious onto the deck.

— Elias Dougal Duran, the boy from the future, 1921
  from *The Confounding Case of Jean-Claude Carré*

The Centrism Decoder Ring

CUT DOTTED LINE

1

BEND GENTLY INTO RING

2

TUCK TABS

3

DISCERN

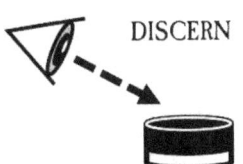

4

FAR RIGHT

Auto-

• Fascist
• Populist
• Conservative

Democracy

• Centrist
• Liberal
• Socialist

cracy

• Communist

FAR LEFT

The
American
Centrist

A Moderate Manifesto

Brent Jones

Table of Contents

Introduction

…politics ought to be the part-time profession of every citizen who would protect the rights and privileges of free people and who would preserve what is good and fruitful in our national heritage.

— Dwight D. Eisenhower, 1954
   Recorded for the Republican Lincoln Day Dinner[1]

Before he looked vaguely like an emaciated mall Santa and when he was still a dapper, clean-shaven comedian hosting *The Daily Show*, Jon Stewart talked a lot about moderate centrism. In one instance, he was opining the lack of enthusiasm for engagement in politics by moderates, and he shouted at his audience with fiery vitriol, *"People! Take to the streets and scream 'BE REASONABLE!'"* He went on to stage a *Million Moderate March* on Washington with Stephen Colbert, which they sardonically dubbed *The Rally to Restore Sanity and/or Fear.*[2] Depending on your perspective, this was either a call-to-arms to centrists everywhere, a liberal stunt of questionable taste, dark comedy, or all of the

---

[1]   Dwight D. Eisenhower, "Address Recorded for the Republican Lincoln Day Dinners," January 28, 1954. https://www.presidency.ucsb.edu/documents/address-recorded-for-the-republican-lincoln-day-dinners

[2]   Amy Goodman, "Jon Stewart and Stephen Colbert Lead Massive Rally to 'Restore Sanity and/or Fear' in DC," *Democracy Now*, November 1, 2010. https://www.democracynow.org/2010/11/1/rally_to_restore_sanity_and_or

above.[3] In any case, it was certainly an illustration of the fractured and divisive state of politics in America. Have things have gotten better or worse in the decade since then? I would assert that the problem is still here, and our political center has not found a voice nor succeeded in demanding reasonableness of the political system.

I remember seeing Stewart's theatrical call for action on the TV, and the premise has grown on me in the years since. Why should centrists who value calm, conversation, collaboration, and compromise not also be passionate? Ultimately, such enthusiasm would really be a passion for democracy itself. If we Americans, the "leaders" of the Free World, can't get excited about democracy, then what in politics should we be excited about?

Well, apparently, quite a lot. The two decades since 9/11 have seen a gradual slide from national unity toward polarization and animosity. Roe v. Wade and Dobbs. The Second Amendment, gun rights, and school shootings. Depravation and deprivation. Discrimination, suffocation, dehumanization, immigration, invasion, escalation, annexation, colonization, conception, abortion, condemnation, restriction, regulation, addiction, allegation, insurrection, assassination, medication, obfuscation, speculation, deception, recession, taxation, sequestration, socialization, mediatization, cancellation, depression,

---

3   Anne Applebaum, "In Praise of Political Compromise," *Slate*, October 25, 2010, 8:02 PM. https://slate.com/news-and-politics/2010/10/jon-stewart-s-million-moderate-march-shows-how-skewed-the-center-has-become.html

demoralization, infection, misinformation, politicization, inoculation, inflation, marginalization, sexualization, emasculation, population, globalization, corporatization, privatization, consumption, legalization, radicalization, defamation, intimidation, capitulation, and liberation.

Depending on your viewpoint, you may have read that list of words with varied reactions. What sprang to mind when you read the word "invasion?" The invasion of Ukraine by Russia? Or perhaps of Israel by Hamas? Or maybe of Gaza by Israel? Or was it tied to "immigration?" I would guess that few readers thought, "Ah, this jerk is trying to be tricky." This is the problem. Our minds have been trained to choose a side rather than to think critically about a political issue and to apply reason to develop an opinion.

So, what do we do about this? This manifesto is one proposal. It suggests centrist principles that we might use to develop our opinions and to judge the candidates for whom we choose to vote. It suggests a moderate way of thinking which attempts to find common ground and to serve the greater good. It highlights changes to the architecture of our political system that would push the country toward the middle rather than toward the extremes. If you find this compelling, then you might write a letter or two to your representatives in government[4] urging them to collaborate and to compromise across the aisle. After all, in the view of the centrist, there is no aisle.

---

[4]   https://www.congress.gov/members/find-your-member
See the back of this manifesto for an example letter or email.

On Human Nature

This is good, but what is best in life?

The open steppe, fleet horse, falcons at your wrist, and the wind in your hair.

Wrong! Conan! What is best in life?

To crush your enemies, see them driven before you, and to hear the lamentations of their women.

That is good! That is good.

— *Conan the Barbarian*[5]

I'll be honest with you—*Conan the Barbarian* is one of my favorite movies, probably second only to *The Princess Bride*. This pinnacle of '80s sword-and-sorcery featured Arnold Schwarzenegger in his physical prime, perfect for Conan, "the damnedest bastard there ever was."[6] But unlike the campy *Beastmaster*, *Ator* the Glamour-Shots himbo, or the ridiculously misogynistic *Deathstalker*, *Conan the Barbarian* is actually an example of artful cinema with a moral center.

---

[5] *Conan the Barbarian*, directed by John Milius, written by John Milius and Oliver Stone, Universal Pictures (1982), based on the literary work of the author Robert E. Howard.
https://www.imdb.com/title/tt0082198/quotes/

[6] *The Whole Wide World*, directed by Dan Ireland, written by Michael Scott Myers, Sony Pictures Classics (1996), based on Novalyne Price Ellis, *One Who Walked Alone,* Donald M. Grant, Publisher, Inc., United States (1986).
https://www.imdb.com/title/tt0118163/quotes/

By the end of the film, Conan learns to trust others, sees the power of love and sacrifice, and brings to ruin a power-hungry extremist cult…and he does it with passionate intensity. For all practical purposes, he is a centrist, when you think about it. And we'll hear from Arnold again later. He'll be back.

This classic *Conan* quote also suggests what may lie at the very base of human nature: a desire for control. The first answer given is essentially *freedom*, but this is rejected by the Mongol general in favor of Conan's articulation of *control*. The instinct for power can be more compelling even than the yearning for freedom. This idea is echoed by a former Disney executive who lists as one of the fundamental human needs "to feel stable and in control."[7] Power over our own environment satisfies the hunger of the foundational and animalistic instinct to survive.

This may not be unique to humans, as the desire for control is certainly present in other intelligent animal species who develop a pecking order within their packs. Adherence to a social hierarchy allows for coordination at a tribal level that can augment the probability of survival for all members of the group.

What, then, does it mean to be human? What sets our species apart from other intelligent animals? We are not unique in employing pack tactics, nor are we unique in

---

7   Meagan Brace, "Imagineering World Class Results," *Sandia Lab News*, September 26, 2019.
     https://www.sandia.gov/labnews/2019/09/26/imagineering/

using our intelligence to project the results of our actions into the future. Anyone who has played fetch with a dog (or a cat) sees that they have a degree of self-awareness and an ability to anticipate. Is it just a matter of degree, or is there something more fundamental? What makes us *human?* Frank Herbert offers a definition:[8]

> *You've heard of animals chewing off a leg to escape a trap? There's an animal kind of trick. A human would remain in the trap, endure the pain, feigning death that he might kill the trapper and remove a threat to his kind.*

A human, then, seeks not only its own survival. It seeks something beyond loyalty to its tribe. It also considers the greater good, and is willing to make a sacrifice of self to achieve it. This is the distinguishing trait that defines a human being.

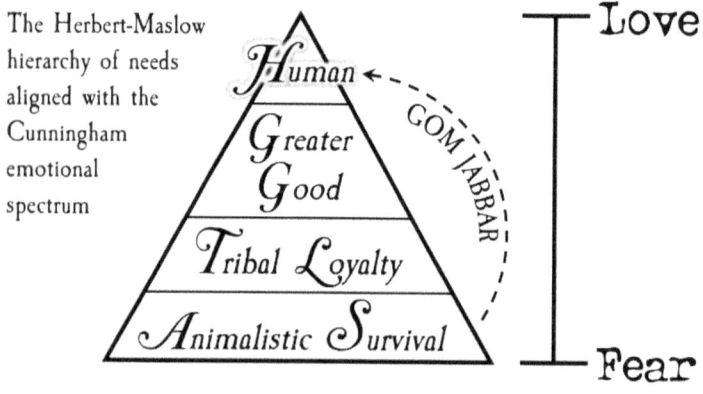

The Herbert-Maslow hierarchy of needs aligned with the Cunningham emotional spectrum

---

8   Frank Herbert, *Dune*, Chilton, Philadelphia and New York (1965).

Now, let's roll this together. The concept of humans having both base-level and higher-order needs is articulated thoughtfully in Maslow's hierarchy of needs.[9] This is drastically simplified, perhaps brutalized, in the diagram shown for the sake of the present discussion, and placed adjacent to it is the Cunningham emotional spectrum.

Here, I am not referring to Don Cunningham, former mayor and CEO from the Lehigh Valley in Pennsylvania. I'll tell you about him later. No, here I am referring to the fictional Jim Cunningham, a motivational speaker with something worse than skeletons in his closet, from the movie *Donnie Darko*.[10] His model is certainly oversimplified—as Donnie points out in the film, there is an enormous range of human emotions that can drive our behaviors—but there can be a grain of truth even in a simple model. Bear with me.

In the world of the novel *Dune*, the sisterhood of the Bene Gesserit uses the technique of pain by nerve induction coupled with the poison needle of the Gom Jabbar to distinguish *humans* from *animals:*[11]

---

[9]   A helpful summary of Maslow's hierarchy of needs can be found at https://www.simplypsychology.org/maslow.html

[10]   *Donnie Darko*, written and directed by Richard Kelly, Newmarket Films (2001).
https://www.imdb.com/title/tt0246578/?ref_=fn_all_ttl_1

[11]   For a cinematic interpretation of the box and the Gom Jabbar, see https://www.youtube.com/watch?v=EHK5fBm1YWk

It kills only animals. Let us say I suggest you may be human. Steady! I warn you not to try jerking away. I am old, but my hand can drive this needle into your neck before you can escape me.

Is the Sisterhood brutal? Yes. *Put your hand in the box*— that's tough love by any accounting. Are they evil? I would argue that they are not. They have the greater good of the entire human species in mind. I'm not endorsing their methods here, mind you, but I am noting their focus on the big picture. In the world I would like to live in, we would have a similar focus, but its implementation would be through kindness, sympathy, and love.

I was always taught that, before you tell me about your religion, first show it to me in terms of how you treat other people. Before you tell me how much you love your God, show it to me in how much you love all of God's children.[12]

Have you ever met someone who is a true and pure Christian? They are rare, in my experience, but I can think of a few that I have met. These are people who approach every relationship they have with another human being with kindness and without judgement. They believe in God's love but they do not push dogma on anyone. Rather, they show this love through how they live. It's in the tone of their voice, in their choice of words, and in their calm demeanor. They make you want to be a better person

---

[12] Sen. Cory Booker on *Inside with Jen Psaki*, *MSNBC*, April 6, 2025. https://archive.org/details/MSNBCW_20250407_020000_Inside_With_Jen_Psaki/start/720/end/780

when you are around them. I would guess that there are similar examples of *humans* from every faith—people who have transcended our animalistic instincts, our tribal loyalties, and have become instruments of the greater good. These are the self-aware and self-actualized individuals who would be sought by the Bene Gesserit.

Politicians understand this Herbert-Maslow hierarchy of needs, at least intuitively if not intellectually. This is where the Cunningham scale enters the discussion. Politicians at their best lift society up on this scale. In the days immediately after 9/11, President George W. Bush brought the nation together with a message of unity and perseverance. In what was to be the pinnacle of his career as a statesman, he took the nation from abject fear to a place of collective resolve. The message of President Barack Obama, which he named Hope, similarly provided a temporal oasis in America's march toward partisan polarization. The country, then, carried itself with a tone of reasonableness. Conservatives did not disappear—their voices were heard on taxation and government spending, national defense, and other matters. But the system worked, and neighbors talked to each other. We cared about each other as Americans. It felt like we were moving together in the same direction.

You know what the other side of this spectrum looks like. We have seen this also in the last few decades.

Unfortunately, the unity following 9/11 wavered in time, and fear entered the political equation once again as the Nation decided to go to war. A naturalized citizen whom

I know commented in the year after 9/11, "I have never seen Americans have so much fear." This comment surprised me at the time, but I could see the truth in it even as it was spoken. This fear affected our collective judgement, and in our uncertainty about the future, we deferred to politicians who presented us with Iraq as an enemy. It can be a comfort to have a known enemy, one that you can seek to defeat. We would almost always rather accept the naming of an enemy over living in the uncertain darkness of an unknown threat. I leave you to judge whether events played out in a way that benefitted our nation and the world, but my observation is that it took us a few years to stabilize emotionally, to refocus on supporting each other, and to see ourselves not as victims of terror but as leaders of the Free World.

Politicians understand the value of fear as a destabilizing force that can shift opinions. Creating fear causes a rapid, irrational, and emotional reassessment to occur. It drives us downward on the Herbert-Maslow hierarchy. We are suddenly worried about our survival, and turn to tribal loyalties as a source of strength and stability. Change in life always brings opportunity, and the shift brought about by fear provides a chance to sway public opinion for the politician willing and able to use it. Fear and chaos are Machiavellian tools that can dislodge those in the center, and when coupled to a "solution" in the form of a grievance and a named enemy, allegiances can solidify or even change.

This trend in electoral politics is discussed in an article published by the American Psychological Association as a compelling and modern phenomenon.[13] This is not new, though. Fear has been tied to politics for millennia. What can we do about it? We can recognize it, we can name it, and we can challenge it. It is up to us to see the emotions invoked in ourselves and to pull ourselves back to reason.

Democracy requires an order that is unnatural to the human species, as Robert E. Howard explains:[14]

> *Barbarism is the natural state of mankind. Civilization is unnatural. It is a whim of circumstance. And barbarism must always ultimately triumph.*

Being a moderate requires conscious effort, then. It demands that we provide an active forcing function to keep our political discourse reasonable and our government balanced at a centrist fulcrum.

Each of us can choose to apply a metaphorical Gom Jabbar to ourselves, wrenching our minds away from our tribal and survival instincts in order to focus on the greater good. This requires overcoming fear, and may require sacrifice or, at the very least, acceptance of risk. You will not always vote for the candidate who promises to benefit your pocketbook the most in the short term, because there are

---

[13] Kirk Waldroff, "Fear: A powerful motivator in elections," *American Psychological Association,* October 22, 2024. https://www.apa.org/news/apa/2020/fear-motivator-elections

[14] Robert E. Howard, "Beyond the Black River," *Weird Tales*, v. 25, nos. 5-6, May-June 1935.

other values at stake, and because we are playing the long game in centrist democracy.

We often hear "Freedom is not free" invoked with respect to military action by the United States. Never was this more true than during the Second World War when our country was a major partner in pushing back the tide of autocracy, but these words should mean more to us beyond a willingness to fight and a call for military readiness. They should also call on us to defend democracy in the public sphere despite social or political pressures in the world. These words demand that we bear the torch of truth and demand integrity from our politicians. They require us to study the issues of the day, to research the candidates for office, and to vote. These words require diligence and attention from all citizens to *protect the rights and privileges of free people.* We must see ourselves as humans, and as centrists, in service of the greater good, and we must answer this call with a fearless and undying passion.

> *You have to carry the fire. ... It's inside you.*
> *It was always there. I can see it.*[15]

We are at a dangerous point in the history of our nation where, as a people, we do not have a common vision of what America should be. Some might say that America stands for freedom, but does that mean *my freedom* or *our freedom*? If you mean *my freedom* then what you really want

---

[15] Cormac McCarthy, *The Road*, Alfred A. Knopf, New York (2006).

is *control*. Some might also say that the great experiment which is the United States has always been at this precipice—hence checks and balances in the Constitution and the assumption of personal greed imbedded implicitly in the structure of free-market capitalism. But do we see the path forward? In this manifesto, I propose that the way forward is cultivating a centrist mindset and shifting the architecture of our political system toward the middle.

In the poem *The Second Coming* by W. B. Yeats, published over a century ago, the author describes the fall of civilization driven by extremists "full of passionate intensity" in which "the centre cannot hold."[16] We need to reverse this, precisely to hold the center. I further propose that centrists everywhere should engage in public discourse and politics with their own passionate intensity, creating in the public consciousness a third path distinct from the left and from the right.

---

16   Thanks to my friend James for making the connection between my thoughts and this poem, which may be found online: https://www.poetryfoundation.org/poems/43290/the-second-coming

Principles of Centrism

If we are to be deliberate in approaching politics from a centrist perspective, then we need a set of principles to help us weigh our decisions. Any approach to human governance is defined both by its theoretical principles and by the policies through which it is implemented. A wise person[17] once said that policies should be self-consistent but principles are often in conflict. The discussion below thus presents guidelines to be kept in mind as we encounter decision gates.

You may not have a black-and-white choice, and your judgement will determine how you weigh your principles, but ensuring that you know your values will lead to clear-eyed decisions. It is how *humans* behave. This is the way. You may see different nuances compared to what is proposed in this manifesto, but if you emerge from the discussion with clarity regarding your own foundational values, then you will come a step closer to mastering the Gom Jabbar…and I'll take that as a measure of success in my own aims for this work.

The Rule of Law

The source of all of the complexity in the physical world, of biological life, and of the rich tapestry of human culture

---

[17] If you know who, let me know the source and I'll cite it…

is...order. Contrary to so many creation myths, our world did not emerge spontaneously out of chaos or nothingness, but was enabled by the detailed structure of the Universe. Sure, the evidence points to a Big Bang and a hot, primordial soup, but it is the physics that governed the cooling of that soup that also led to the emergence of life. The balance of energy and matter allowed stars and planets to form. Quantum mechanics led to the structure of atoms that can support chemical bonds, leading eventually to the emergence of DNA. It is hard to deny that we owe our life on this drifting, slippery rock to the particular laws that govern how all things interact. If you believe in God, then you might say this was God's law. If not, you would call it the laws of Nature. They might be the same thing, but in any case, the rule of law underpins the Universe.

In studies of system theory, a *generative framework* is any simple set of rules that leads to complex, and often amazing, emergent behavior. The way that birds flock or fish school appears to come from a higher intelligence, but essentially is the result of the biological coding that has evolved in these individual organisms. The Mandelbrot set is another example, the esoteric and enchanting fractal pattern that flickered onto computer screens in 1980 and then into the public consciousness. A simple equation and a set of rules for iteration leads to seemingly infinite complexity. Our brains are built with biological neurons, the original building block of consciousness on Earth. They similarly follow a set of foundational rules for how each interacts with the other, and this leads to incredible perceptive, computational, and creative power. Generative AI is fundamentally no different. We often think of complex and emergent behavior as chaotic, but even chaos sits upon a foundation of order. The yin cannot exist without the yang. And the complex soup that emerges can be savory…or sometimes bitter.

The same is true in political systems—there must always be a foundation based on order. In our country, it is the Constitution of the United States of America that provides the fundamental rules for the function of government, including its authorities and its limitations. Without a foundation based on order, a society can exist only in Robert E. Howard's state of barbarism. The legislative code that has been built on top of the Constitution for over two centuries is the emergent result of the generative framework created by the Founders of the Nation.

In America today, many people have lost faith in the function of the federal government and our national political system. This brings us to the present problem—some of these people would rather tear it all down rather than do the work to improve the system. In an interview with Fareed Zakaria, David Brooks commented on recent trends in which political appointees and elected officials increasingly carry allegations or convictions of harassment, abuse, or corruption as part of their identities. What once would have ended a political career has become, for some voters, a mark of credibility. Brooks explains:[18]

---

[18] David Brooks on Fareed Zakaria, *Global Public Square*, *CNN*, December 22, 2024, 10:00 ET. https://transcripts.cnn.com/show/fzgps/date/2024-12-22/segment/01

And there are large majorities in this country, not just Republicans, who think the systems are fundamentally broken. We need somebody who's going to come in and break the rules. ...these people who have all these scandals, that's a virtue, not a vice, because if they have scandals, that shows they're rule breakers.

Look, I get it. It absolutely feels like the system is broken. Let's just talk about the Congressional budgeting process for a second. The United States of America has not passed a full budget on time (that is, without a Continuing Resolution) since 1997.[19] I will tell you from my professional experience that this creates uncertainty for project managers which then reduces the efficiency and effectiveness of efforts that the government chooses to support, and, frankly, is a significant detriment to national security. But is the solution to tear it all down?

Tyrion Lannister: It's a beautiful dream, stopping the wheel. You're not the first person who's ever dreamt it.

Daenerys Targaryen: I'm not going to stop the wheel, I'm going to break the wheel.[20]

---

[19] Drew C. Aherne *et al.*, "Continuing Resolutions: Overview of Components and Practices," *Congressional Research Service Product R46595, U.S. Library of Congress,* March 27, 2025. https://www.congress.gov/crs-product/R46595

[20] *Game of Thrones,* "Hardhome," directed by Miguel Sapochnik, written by David Benioff and D. B. Weiss, *HBO* (2015). https://www.imdb.com/title/tt3866850/quotes/

But what happens when you try to break the wheel? Cities are scorched by dragon fire and people die. You may be thinking that *Game of Thrones* is just a story, it's not real. No, but art imitates life and at its best captures a kernel of wisdom for our reflection. You might also be thinking that there are those who are trying to break the wheel in America right now. How is that going for everyone? Polarization, divisiveness, ineffectual governance, anger, and fear are what I see emerging.

I am a firm believer in working within the system. When my kids complain about mom and dad asking them to be home at nine o'clock, or whatever, I pull the "work within the system" card out of my pocket. This can include voting, lobbying, protest, litigation, or legislation but it does not include breaking the law. If you don't like the rules, then work to change the rules. Build a network of relationships that allows you to have influence. Work with likeminded people to push your policy objectives ahead. Work with people who have conflicting views to find common ground and champion those issues together. Spoiler alert: This is exactly what Tyrion Lannister did at the conclusion to *A Game of Thrones*. Once more from David Brooks: [21]

> *As we've seen over and over again down the centuries, there's a big difference between people who operate in the spirit of disruption and those who operate in the spirit of reform.*

---

[21] David Brooks, "How Trump will Fail," *The New York Times*, January 23, 2025.
https://www.nytimes.com/2025/01/23/opinion/trump-mckinley-populism.html

To be clear, we should absolutely seek change and do it with a passionate intensity. But for the centrist, this should be done with a respect for the rule of law, with change emerging from within the system. America has reinvented itself many times over the centuries, with cultural shifts accompanied by legislation. While it can seem broken (and I guarantee you that it has to many generations over the last two-and-a-half centuries) the fabric of American governance has held strong and adapted as the underpinning of democracy through the Civil War, through the Great Depression, and through other times of trial. We need to recognize that rule of law is in our best interest, even as we exercise our free speech to protest and to vote for change.

True, our country was born in the fire and bloodshed of the American Revolution, which at face value does not follow the principle of "work within the system," but this was an exceptional circumstance involving the struggle against a tyrannical monarchy. Beginning with the adoption of the Constitution and the Bill of Rights, we now have a framework that guarantees the freedoms of the individual, limits the power of government with checks and balances, and has proven to be a generative framework capable of enabling the evolution and reinvention of the most prosperous country in the world. We should vote for politicians who mean it when they take an oath to uphold the Constitution of the United States. This is the first pillar of the American centrist.

Beginning in Great Britain in the mid-1700's, the Industrial Revolution brought rapid changes in automation which spread through all corners of society. As with every leap forward in technology, it widened the gap between the rich and the poor. The formerly agrarian lifestyle of many gave way to the economic juggernaut of automated manufacturing at a scale that only the wealthy capitalists could afford. While ultimately industrialization would raise the global standard of living, prolong life expectancy, and reduce infant mortality, the urban living conditions of factory workers were in many cases appalling and oppressive in the early phase of this revolution.

Utilitarianism was a response to these conditions, as society grappled with what morality should look like in this new age. Jeremy Bentham, often credited as the father of utilitarianism, summed it up concisely: [22]

> *The greatest happiness of the greatest number is the foundation of morals and legislation.*

Bentham's thoughts on this were first put to paper as, "it is the greatest happiness of the greatest number that is the measure of right and wrong," in *A Fragment on Government*, written in 1776.[23] That date should sound familiar. The

---

[22] Jeremy Bentham, *The Commonplace Book, Collected Works* (1774-5). https://utilitarianism.net/utilitarian-quotes/

[23] James E. Crimmins, "Jeremy Bentham," *The Stanford Encyl. of Philosophy* (2021). https://plato.stanford.edu/entries/bentham/

values associated with utilitarianism were already entering the Western zeitgeist as the founders of our nation made the challenging decision to break from England and pursue democracy. The language also evokes the Declaration of Independence itself, which states that "the pursuit of Happiness" is an unalienable right.

The second pillar of American centrism, then, is utilitarianism. The pursuit of the greater good. Per our earlier discussion on human nature, this is what distinguishes us from *animal*, defines being *human*, and is the bar that we must hold up for ourselves, for politicians, and for our government.

The day after the 2024 election, my sixteen-year-old son and I were getting breakfast in the kitchen and discussing the results of the previous night. He told me, "Dad, I think people were just thinking about what was best for themselves and their families, and it seems like that is a good thing."

There is no question that we all think about our families first. It is a product of the evolution of the human species. Loyalty to our tribe is part of what helped our ancestors to survive in a world full of mortal threats, but it is also more than that. Caring for those closest to us gives us fulfillment, and is a fundamental value of every human culture. It is one of the very best aspects of being human. So, he is not wrong...but that cannot be the end of the story.

Human civilization has grown in its breadth and depth over five millennia of recorded history. It has achieved a richness and a beauty that demands of us as sentient humans to think beyond the boundaries of family and tribe. Society is so interconnected, we cannot think of our family in opposition to and in competition with all others. We need to broaden our definition of tribe to encompass the Nation if not the world. Not to do so would mean national infighting, polarization, fear, hatred, and, if I want to be dramatic, ultimately the downfall of civilization.

One goal that I have in writing this book is to convince my son to think more broadly than just what is best for "me and my family." We need to balance the priority of taking care of our families with the imperative of the good of the many. We may even need to be willing to sacrifice our own interests to uphold our greater principles. If we do not, then we cannot expect compassion toward us in our own time of need, and we cannot expect our country to be strong. This is utilitarianism in its most essential form.

We also have to recognize that utilitarianism is not an absolute goal. Taken to the extreme, it becomes socialism and then communism. No communist government has ever survived reality. Every instance in modern history has morphed into autocracy with the rights and the freedoms of the people curtailed. In a democracy, the danger to watch out for with utilitarianism is the tyranny of the majority. This brings us to the next principle of centrism, the need to respect others and to consider their rights as a foundational element in weighing the greater good.

Respect Others

That which you do to the least of my brothers,
you do unto me.

— Jesus of Nazareth, Matthew 25:40

Treating the less fortunate well is akin to treating Jesus well, but we can also consider the inverse. To treat the less fortunate poorly is to treat Jesus poorly. This verse captures the Christian moral imperative to treat others with respect, kindness, and compassion.

I am not a great Christian, I will be the first to tell you. I was raised Catholic, but drifted away as an adult as it seemed so hard to reconcile a scientific and evidence-based view of the world with a faith-based, religious view. It's not impossible to hold faith and science together. Logic is always based on fundamental assumptions about truths within Nature, and science may never answer questions such as, "Why does the Universe exist?" or, "What came before that?" There is always a hole in the bottom which logic cannot fill. Faith and spirituality are a part of the human experience, even for scientists who marvel at complexity in Nature and how often the whole seems to transcend the sum of its parts. An even greater pragmatic concern and frustration with organized religion, however, has been the imprint of institutionalized power structures onto faith that creeps into every Church, and the tribalism and violence that can too often be enabled by religions. I still wrestle with that and continue to find it hard to embrace the structure of a Church in my adult life.

23

All that said, I found myself getting a little emotional in talking about the words of Jesus in a conversation one day with my kids on faith and religion. Perhaps it was some deeply imbedded resonance from my Catholic upbringing, or some deeper-still thread of human nature. The most compelling part of the New Testament, I told them, is the encounter between Jesus and the Pharisees in which they seek to entrap him by asking which of the Ten Commandments is the most important. His answer is brilliant. Of course it is.

You shall love the Lord your God with all your heart and with all your soul and with all your mind. This is the great and first commandment. And a second is like it: You shall love your neighbor as yourself. On these two commandments depend all the Law and the Prophets.

— Jesus of Nazareth, Matthew 22:37-40

That just about sums up the whole Bible—all you need to go with it is a clear understanding of the definition of God and how God interacts with the Universe, and you are all set. But read the second of these Great Commandments one more time. We all know this. We teach this to our kindergartners in every generation. It is foundational to sharing, to empathy, to seeking the greater good beyond yourself or your tribe.

We also state this Great Commandment as a secular value in several forms:

The Golden Rule

Treat others as you would like to be treated.

The Platinum Rule

Treat others as they would like to be treated.

The Diamond Rule

Treat others as they need to be treated.

It blew my mind when I first heard of the Platinum and Diamond extensions to the well-known Golden Rule, but, fundamentally, these variations are all forms of saying that we should respect others and care about them. If we adopt this as a fundamental imperative, then this builds on and complements the principle of pursuing the greater good, but it adds a crucial modification.

The flaw with pursing only simple utilitarianism without the nuances of respect and compassion is that it can lead to a tyranny of the majority. If we seek "the greatest happiness of the greatest number," then is it perfectly fine if the happiness and the rights of a small minority are sacrificed to obtain it? Does that still fulfill our notion of a greater good? The answer is no. An essential part of our democracy is that individuals have fundamental, unalienable, and now *Constitutional* rights. We can't all be free unless we respect each other's freedom, and this requires at least tolerance if not compassion. It requires that we overcome our survival instinct to name a minority as the "other" and then to trample their rights when we face fear and uncertainty ourselves.

This is then the third pillar of American centrism: Respect others, and be vigilant against the tyranny of the majority. We must challenge ourselves and our society when the will of a majority begins to violate the fundamental rights of minority populations. This principle demands that we examine our motivations deeply whenever we consider accepting an action that limits the rights of others. Are we really seeking the greater good, or are we just acting as animals in a state of fear?

It is worth saying a few words about longtermism,[24] the modern extension of utilitarianism that spreads its philosophical reach across the long axis of time. The most basic tenets of longtermism are admirable. It demands that we think of future generations when we consider the greater good. It echoes of the Seven Generations Principle from America's indigenous Haudenosaunee Confederacy, which states that leaders, "must not think only of themselves, their families, or even their immediate communities. Instead, they must consider the well-being of those who will come after them."[25] Long-term planning

---

[24] Longtermism.com, "What is longtermism?" (2021).
      https://longtermism.com/
[25] Breanne Smith, "Seven Generations Principle: Healing the Past & Shaping the Future," *The Indigenous Foundation*.

is something that we need more of in our society, which is too often dominated by annual earnings reports and twenty-four-hour news cycles.

But longtermism takes this further, asserting that humanity will endure for eons, with countless human lives yet to be born whose worth is each as great as our own. The conclusion drawn by longtermists is that the well-being of the future greatly outweighs that of the present. This can be dangerous when combined with the additional assertion that the consequences of our actions are predictable over these vast time scales. Why dangerous? For the same reason that The Diamond Rule makes me nervous. How confident are you that you know what is best for someone else, especially if you act to constrain their freedoms against their wishes? Likewise, it may be hubris to think that we can predict and control the future of humanity accurately enough to value generations of the distant future above those alive today.

Longtermism has established a following among tech billionaires who, in some cases, are willing to spend enormous sums of money toward creating a future to benefit these distant generations.[26] This might be a really good idea, especially if the benefits can be felt in the near term—perhaps as far as seven generations forward—

---

https://www.theindigenousfoundation.org/articles/seven-generations-principle-healing-the-past-amp-shaping-the-future

[26] Émile P Torres, "Against Longtermism," *Aeon* (2021), https://aeon.co/essays/why-longtermism-is-the-worlds-most-dangerous-secular-credo

though I have a sneaking suspicious that there is an element of the fear of death and the quest for immortality in these billionaire ventures.

If a longtermist is willing to sacrifice the good of the people living today to achieve their aims, then we have a problem if in fact the span of human control will not extend reliably for millennia. And I don't see how it can.

It is difficult to make predictions, especially about the future.

— Niels Bohr, Yogi Berra, or Nostradamus[27]

Chaos theory and the butterfly effect warn that miniscule changes in initial conditions can lead to vastly different outcomes in the long term—a butterfly flapping its wings in Brazil can lead to a hurricane on the Eastern Seaboard. We can't even predict the stock market, election outcomes, or fidget-spinner trends a year from now.

The trap associated with a complete willingness to sacrifice the present in favor of the future is one of making the perfect the enemy of the good. If society were to sacrifice the present generation perpetually so as to work toward a magnificent but distant future, then we may never achieve a positive outcome for anyone. This is a case of a tyranny of the majority, where the majority in this scenario is the hypothetically enormous population of the extended

---

[27] quoteresearch, "Quote Origin: It's Difficult to Make Predictions, Especially About the Future," *The Quote Investigator*, October 20, 2013. https://quoteinvestigator.com/2013/10/20/no-predict/

future, and those of us alive on the Earth today then become the suppressed minority.

A healthy combination of utilitarianism, foresight, and empathy could augment the greater good in the present and (ambitiously) for seven generations to come, even as we think seventy generations ahead and lay the foundation for the future of humanity. But we must be pragmatic. Seeking to eliminate polio from the world[28] is enormously admirable. Such an achievement would help people tangibly today and forever into the future. That's compassionate long-term thinking. I find the prospect of extending humanity to other worlds, starting with a trip to Mars,[29] to be exciting and inspiring. It is one step removed from helping people today, but it fuels the imagination and is already leading to innovation in spaceflight. The idea that human minds will be resurrected through a massive AI system imbedded in a Dyson sphere encompassing a star[30] is…well, I'm sorry, but that is just absolutely bonkers. It is so far skewed toward the long term that it loses sight of the people of today. This is the flaw with strong longtermism, and the crack through which cold cruelty can

28   The Gates Foundation, "Polio" (2025). https://www. gatesfoundation.org/our-work/programs/global-development/polio

29   SpaceX, "Mars & Beyond: The Road to Making Humanity Multiplanetary" (2025).
https://www.spacex.com/humanspaceflight/mars

30   Matthew Griffin, "New Transhumanist theory thinks Dyson Spheres could unlock human immortality," *Earth and Energy* (2021). https://www.311institute.com/new-transhumanist-theory-thinks-dyson-spheres-could-unlock-human-immortality/

slip into intellectual erudition and emergent reasoning. Remember grandma's saying: Balance in all things…which leads to the next principle proposed in this centrist manifesto.

Manage Tensions

In nature, the optimum is almost always in the middle somewhere. Distrust assertions that the optimum is at an extreme point.

— Akin's Eighth Law of Spacecraft Design[31]

Like the Seven Rules of Admiral Rickover, Akin's laws have been repeated and recast in a multitude of forms throughout the blogosphere. They are each their own gems of wisdom, but this particular law has always stood out to me, and it is particularly relevant to the present discussion.

Any manager of people or of programs will learn within the first year of their job that there are many things that must be held in tension. Is it better to have formality of operations at a high-hazard facility, or do you want to rely on the experience and skill of the workers? Each has their place. Should researchers be free to explore topics they are passionate about, or should they be directed toward

---

[31]   David Akin, "Akin's Laws of Spacecraft Design," *University of Maryland* (2022).
https://web.archive.org/web/20220310210342/https://spacecraft.ssl.umd.edu/akins_laws.html

mission work? Both, and if you can find an overlap in these, then you will maximize productivity and retention. Likewise, in society, should we have an economy based on free-market capitalism, or should government regulation play a role? Are traditional values the way to go, or should we embrace modern ideals? Should we plan for the future or live for today?

The answer to all of these is *both* and *neither*. We must find a solution in the middle, one that is developed including dialogue with stakeholders. Those at the extremes may not like the solution, but it is role of the centrist to push back against extremism, to seek the greater good, and to articulate the reason for doing so cogently. And when a solution is found, the work is not done. Managing tensions is a perpetual calling.[32] The fourth pillar of American centrism is then: distrust extremes, find a solution in the middle, and be willing to compromise.

Barry Johnson has published a system for thinking through problems involving tensions of this sort. He calls it Polarity Management,[33] and it provides useful tools for introspection, finding common values, and developing solutions. We will return to this tool later in the manifesto, but it is worth mentioning here Dr. Johnson's analogy to breathing as a cycle or a spectrum between extremes.

---

[32] Lyssa Adkins, "Rules, Principles and Tensions to Hold" (2020). https://www.linkedin.com/pulse/rules-principles-tensions-hold-lyssa-adkins-she-her

[33] Barry Johnson, *Polarity Management: Identifying and Managing Unsolvable Problems*. HRD Press (1996).

When we breathe in, we take in fresh oxygen needed for life. But we can't only breathe in. Breathing out has its upsides too, including expelling waste carbon dioxide and freeing lung volume for more oxygen. Any proponent of inhaling or exhaling will recognize certain common goals, such as managing blood oxygen levels and remaining alive. The best solution will come by listening to each other's hopes and fears, and then working together to develop a path forward. We will agree to implement it together, to keep talking about how it is going, and to iterate and refine the solution as a team.

By managing the polarity in a process continually, we reap the benefits of the upsides and minimize the downsides. In fact, the benefits of managing a polarity well are to dampen the swing between extremes and to keep the entire process nearer to the benefits we collectively want and away from the negative outcomes we fear.

In my professional life, as mentioned, I applied this approach to thinking through management of high-hazard research facilities, where we often see tension between those who seek formal operations with detailed written procedures and training programs versus those who want to rely on the deep experience of skilled workers. One camp seeks agility and fears being hamstrung by paperwork, while the other seeks stability and fears losing key expertise and knowledge that was never written down.

The best result comes if the two sides listen to each other and adopt a hybrid approach. Formal documentation can be used in exceptionally high-hazard, high-consequence work with many interfaces between teams. Skill of the worker is best suited for daily operations within a standard hazard envelope where the research-and-development needs of the facility require constant adaptation to new experimental configurations. After all, we all agree on common goals. We want world-class, high-quality data, we want workers to go home safely, and we want the facility operations to be efficient and sustainable.

I shared this perspective in a lunchtime seminar, and the response was overwhelmingly positive. While it was not at all my focus in that venue, members of the audience immediately saw the connection to America's political climate too. People are so used to choosing a side and ruminating on their fears of the detriments that will come if the other side wins. It can be a revelation to change your mindset to study the entire spectrum, to identify common goals, and to propose a path forward together.

In the realm of politics, the American centrist sits at the principal pivot point of polarity management. It is the centrist who must reach out to those on the extremes and actively pull them to the middle, toward common goals and the greater good. If the Republicans and the Democrats won't breathe, then the independent centrists will need to do it for the Nation. We need to apply the political equivalent of CPR, get people to the table, and push policy and legislation to the middle. And, in case I didn't mention it, the work is never done.

One last comment on managing tensions: Listening is required. I will admit to you that listening is a weak area for me personally. I'm sure that my wife and coworkers would agree on this point. I tend to sink within the roiling depths of my own mind, and, once I emerge with what I think is a good idea, I fixate on it and it can be hard for me to listen to other perspectives. It's how my brain works. I may be worse than average, but I actually think that a deficiency of quality listening is not uncommon in our species. It takes an intentional action to snap out of this mode. When frustration appears on the face of your conversation partner, that needs to be a red flag that you should stop talking and think about listening. It's like exercising a muscle, and it takes practice. You may not always be successful, but actively listening as part of managing tensions and developing that skill is a continuous action item for the American centrist. I'm still working on it myself.

Use of Evidence

We spoke earlier about order and natural law as the foundation of all emergent behavior in the Universe. This is a deep philosophical perspective, and is certainly core to the scientific method. A scientist will form a hypothesis based on the fundamental assumption that there are rules governing the behavior of Nature, that these rules are consistent and immutable, and that a well-posed experiment performed (and repeated by anyone) can test that hypothesis and help to reveal truth about the Universe. The method of the scientist is really just the method of any reasonable person who uses logic and evidence to draw conclusions. This is also the fifth pillar of the American centrist: Use of evidence enables wise decisions.

This seems so simple, but it is a point of which modern society has started to lose sight within the complexity and turbulence of the digital world. I was talking with my kids about social media and where people are getting their news these days. We've all heard it and read about it—the online echo chambers and one-sided news sources are a significant contributor to polarization in America. The early promise of the internet as a means of sharing information and bringing people together has been twisted by the stove-piped architectures and algorithms of social media apps. Instead of being connected digitally, we may be more divided and isolated than ever.

I was surprised by the response from my kids in this discussion. "But Dad, it's all just opinion. All you can do is to decide whose opinion you want to believe in."

There are some who say that perception is king. It is certainly true that perception matters enormously in how decisions are made, and every organization relying on external funding in a competitive environment better have a darn good public relations strategy. But perception is NOT truth. Centrists need to push back on this point *hard*.

Let me elaborate on this in two parts, one on respecting truth and one on trusting experts.

> *My father once told me that respect for truth comes close to being the basis for all morality. 'Something cannot emerge from nothing,' he said. This is profound thinking if you understand how unstable 'the truth' can be.*

— The Princess Irulan, Bene Gesserit sister and daughter of the Padishah Emperor Shaddam IV[8]

There is truth in the Universe, and evidence and reason can reveal it. This needs to be a core belief of the centrist.

The online environment has become wickedly polarized, and information presented often has a bias, a messaging intent, and is constructed in order to drive a certain narrative. It might be advertising, or it might be politics, but both play off of our fears and our desires. My kids recognized this in their comment that "it's all just opinion."

But I can't accept that, and neither should you. It is possible to obtain factual information. It is not just all opinion. Real news outlets use original sources and fact-check themselves. Real technical experts subject their own work to peer review, and expect the same of others. Extraordinary claims demand extraordinary proof, and an engineer or scientist might retest and challenge prior experimental results, seeking corroborating data or a reduction in statistical uncertainty to support a conclusion.

Underlying all of this is the fundamental principle that there is an absolute truth and that we can uncover it with appropriate evidence and analysis. It is not a matter of opinion how many people died from COVID or whether the vaccine causes health complications. It is not a matter of opinion what data are recorded to inform an analysis of leading economic indicators. We can and should demand evidence, but, at the end of the day, those things are facts. Policy and legislation are opinion, essentially, but if they are done well then they must be based on evidence.

> *The first principle is that you must not fool yourself— and you are the easiest person to fool.*

> — Richard Feynman, *Cargo Cult Science* [34]

In addition to requiring evidence to support decisions, we must be mindful of the sources of that evidence. We must seek unbiased sources of information, to the extent that that is possible, and we must recognize the residual biases that will always be present.

When I vote, I always do some modicum of research in advance on the candidates, bond issues, state constitutional amendments, and everything else on the ballot. It's a civic duty for "*every citizen who would protect the rights and privileges of free people,*" as President Eisenhower said. I look at the local TV stations and newspapers, but one of the sources I value the most is the League of Women Voters guide for my

---

[34]   Richard Feynman, "Cargo Cult Science,"
       Caltech commencement address (1974),
       https://calteches.library.caltech.edu/51/2/CargoCult.htm

state.[35] The League has a history dating back to the days of the women's suffrage movement and today is active in voting rights and communication. Their guide prints statements that the candidates themselves have written and submitted. They often publish statements for and against bond questions and constitutional amendments. Their agenda is simply to share information and to inform the voting public. It's about as unbiased as you can get.

The daily news cycle is harder. I listen to MSNBC (now MSNOW), NPR, CNN, and Fox News regularly. My wife likes Reuters, which is rated as one of the most centrist and objective media outlets.[36] She might forward me an article from the Wall Street Journal or from the New York Times. If you are not looking across the spectrum and you are deciding to trust only one news source, then you are not seeing the full picture. In cases where evidence is not easily made quantitative, you must seek multiple sources of information. You must seek truth actively and demand higher-quality information, especially when it really counts, such as during elections or times of national crisis.

Try this exercise for yourself. If you lean politically to the right, listen to MSNBC for twenty minutes. If you lean left, listen to Fox News. Your first reaction to the spin doctors will probably be, "This is absolute horse turds." But don't turn the channel just yet. Think about the fact

---

[35] https://www.lwvcnm.org/ You can find your local LWV chapter here: https://www.lwv.org/local-leagues/find-local-league
[36] AllSides, "AllSides Media Bias Chart" (2025).
https://www.allsides.com/media-bias/media-bias-chart

that somewhere out there, someone else from the other side of the political spectrum is doing the same thing that you are. They are upset by the language and framing that you are generally more comfortable with. When the twenty minutes are up, ask yourself the following questions:

Questions to Challenge your Perspective
Which of my values are leading me to be upset by what I am hearing?
What values or emotions is this other perspective appealing to?
What common beliefs do I have with someone who holds this other perspective?
What could I say to them to help them to understand my values and feelings?
What question could I ask them to help me to understand their feelings and values?
Which common goals could I work on together with someone from this other perspective?

There are a range of perspectives always present in the sphere of legitimate news sources. You need to do some regular sampling and hold a seek-to-understand attitude if you want to discern the truth and to understand the perceptions held by others. Be mindful that half of America is listening to MSNBC and half to Fox News. You need to hear these perspectives for yourself and do the work to discern the underlying truth. If you are only listening to one news source, then you are missing at least half of the discourse.

And, by the way, social media does not provide high-quality news sources. In addition to the risk of misinformation through bots and propaganda from hostile foreign entities, social media may pose a real danger to our young people.

> *In Australia, they banned social media for under 16 because they saw the research. This is devastating to our children's brains. We're in the biggest brain and mental health epidemic in history.*
>
> — Dr. Daniel Amen[37]

My kids are constantly fed politically-slanted ads and reposts, and it's not good. You should ask your kids about what they are seeing online. Seeking truth and being media savvy needs to start early in life, and should be a kitchen-table discussion topic between kids and parents across the nation.

---

[37] Fox & Friends Weekend, Fox News, September 13, 2025. I am unable to locate a link to a transcript for this quote online, but a useful discussion of social media and children can be found here: https://www.yalemedicine.org/news/social-media-teen-mental-health-a-parents-guide

Trust Experts

I always say you should know your strengths and listen to the experts. If you want to learn about building biceps, listen to me, because I've spent my life studying how to get the perfect peak and I have been called the greatest bodybuilder of all time. We all have different specialties.

Dr. Fauci and all of the virologists and epidemiologists and doctors have studied diseases and vaccines for their entire lives, so I listen to them and I urge you to do the same. None of us are going to learn more than them by watching a few hours of videos. It's simple: if your house is on fire, you don't go on YouTube, you call the damn fire department. If you have a heart attack, you don't check your Facebook group, you call an ambulance. If 9 doctors tell you you have cancer and need to treat it or you will die, and 1 doctor says the cancer will disappear, you should always side with the 9. In this case, virtually all of the real experts around the world are telling us the vaccine is safe and some people on Facebook are saying it isn't.

In general, I think if the circle of people you trust gets smaller and smaller and you find yourself more and more isolated, it should be a warning sign that you're going down a rabbit hole of misinformation. Some people say it is weak to listen to experts. That's bogus. It takes strength to admit you don't know everything. Weakness is thinking you don't need expert advice and only listening to sources that confirm what you want to believe.

— Arnold Schwarzenegger, 2021[38]

[38] Dan Evon, "Did Schwarzenegger Urge People to Trust Experts on COVID-19?" *Snopes* (2021), https://www.snopes.com/fact-check/schwarzenegger-covid-experts/

I just told you to use evidence in making decisions, but none of us can be experts in everything. From a pragmatic perspective, to enable ourselves and our society to function, we will have to place trust in others opinions, especially on matters of great impact where the knowledge of a specialist is required. Even scientists and engineers do this—they trust the work of colleagues in order to build on it and to accelerate the progress of the team. Sometimes this can lead to error, but, through peer review and repeated experimentation, the truth inevitably comes to light. The Governator (I told you he'd be back) talked about relying on doctors and fire fighters, and we are faced with making judgements on the expertise of many other people and institutions that affect our lives.

The critical factor here is to decide where and how to place your trust when it is necessary to do so. It should never be based on charisma. That's the path to the dark side. When you read between the lines and look under the hood, charismatic peddlers of opinion use assertion and wordplay to be convincing. They have no real credibility and their arguments are not based on sound evidence nor on thoughtful analysis. You need to find experts who have invested deeply in understanding the evidence, who are transparent in sharing the data along with their analysis and reasoning in a way that you can follow, and whose reputations are linked to the accuracy of their facts, the thoroughness of their analysis, and the quality of their conclusions.

One expert source that I trust in local voting is my state's Judicial Performance Evaluation Commission.[39] They utilize experts to perform a nonpartisan and objective rating of the efficacy of the judges who are on the ballot. Without this source of expert opinion, I would not have enough information to vote on retention of judges. Now, if a judge were in the news for bad behavior (or for exceptional behavior), then I would add that evidence to the calculus. I will have to monitor this commission over time, and if I ever read of ethical concerns in their process, then I will have to reevaluate my trust.

Eternal vigilance is the price of freedom.

Freedom is not free.

Yo, Adrian.

---

[39] New Mexico Judicial Performance Evaluation Commission, https://nmjpec.org/en/faq

A Centrist Platform

Major flaws in government arise from a fear of making radical internal changes even though a need is clearly seen.

— Darwi Odrade, Reverend Mother of the Bene Gesserit[40]

We have discussed the rule of law and warned against the breaking of the wheel, but that does not mean that bold change should not be pursued. All organizations suffer from the growing cancer of bureaucracy over time, a creeping kudzu of administrative obfuscation that makes governance less efficient and less effective. Furthermore, political parties and other powers have a way of bending government to their own benefit. The United States of America has had a quarter of a millennium for these forces to work against the greater good. It is not hard to find common ground on the need for reform, but…where to start? What issues should be the focal point of the centrist in order to provide a counterforce against entropy and corruption, to demand radical change that would favor the people of this country?

Here is a list, kept short and simple by intent. None of these are ideological hot topics that divide the right and the left. All are focused on democracy and creating structure

---

[40]   Frank Herbert, *Chapterhouse: Dune,* G.P. Putnam's Sons, New York (1985).

in our government which would reinforce reasonableness and deemphasize the extremes. We need this urgently. A significant part of the reason for such divisiveness today is that the architecture of government has been prodded and bent so severely by politicians, parties, corporations, and demagogues over the centuries that our legal framework is now nearly incapable of protecting the center. We live in a house with a solid foundation, but whose timbers are rotting and infested. It's time to remodel.

"The door is wide open for extremes on both ends of the political spectrum," said Harry Enten on a cable news program entitled, "Are the extremes taking over American politics?"[41] The premise was that people are fed up, want change, and the extremes feel like an anti-establishment haven. It's the same point we heard from David Brooks.[18] We need to change that mindset, and convince Americans not to flee to the extremes but to fight for the middle.

If independent voters supported this centrist platform as a top priority, we could vote out politicians who are partisan or extremist. Remember that the independent centrists are the fulcrum of the electorate. If we demand culture change and legislation to reinforce centrism in America, the ultimate result would be a government that answers to the common good. Manipulation of the political system would not be tolerated, those politicians who crossed the line

---

[41] "Are the extremes taking over American politics?" *Table for Five*, hosted by Abby Phillip, *CNN*, June 28, 2025. https://transcripts.cnn.com/show/se/date/2025-06-28/segment/01

would lose their seats, and the forcing function would be toward the center rather than toward political parties who seek power above all else. Think hard about this centrist platform and about the past actions of candidates on the ballot the next time you vote.

Uphold Voting Rights

I would contend that it was always the wish of America's Founding Fathers to guarantee the fundamental rights of life, liberty, and the pursuit of happiness to all humans in this country who think, hope, laugh, cry, strive, and love. But they were constrained by the ethics, mores, and norms of their times, as are we all (not to mention economics and the influence of political powers). To quote one physicist that I know, "Most of us do the best we can,"[42] or to quote one comedian, "You can't do better—if you could, you would."[43] The Three-Fifths Compromise is the best they could come up with, and I don't mean that in a pejorative sense. The Founders struggled with the ideals of freedom and democracy and then did what they were able to do.

But buried deep within the Nation's soul, we all knew what the intention was. Freedom. Some feared it—a fear of change and loss, really—but we knew. The question of freedom boiled up to the surface in the Civil War, then came the Emancipation Proclamation, Juneteenth, Reconstruction, and Jim Crow. Still we struggled. Women

---

[42] Robert J. Commisso, U.S. Naval Research Laboratory.
[43] Jerry Seinfeld, Kiva Auditorium, Albuquerque, NM (2024).

suffragists reminded us, the 19th Amendment was ratified at the start of the Roaring Twenties, then women hit glass ceilings. Still we struggled. Black Americans reminded us again in the Civil Rights Era, the Voting Rights Act was signed into law in 1965,[44] then MLK was killed.

We are still struggling with the question of freedom today, but voting rights is simple from the perspective of the American centrist. In a representative democracy, the people must be represented. To be represented, the elections must be free and fair, and citizens must vote. Apathy is a chronic archenemy of the centrist, but active suppression of citizens' right to vote is the utter antithesis of democracy. To be clear, this is not a liberal issue—this is a centrist issue. It is about keeping strength in the center of the political spectrum and power with the electorate.

We just passed the 60th anniversary of the Voting Rights Act, and still disenfranchisement of minority voters is in the news.[45] It used to be poll taxes and literacy tests, refusal to register voters and physical violence against Black Americans. Now it is voting rule changes, litigation, reinterpretation of the Constitution, and redistricting fights (more on that in the next section). So this is the first plank in the platform of the American centrist: Uphold and

---

44 Voting Rights Act (1965), *National Archives of the U.S.A.* https://www.archives.gov/milestone-documents/voting-rights-act

45 John Kruzel and Andrew Chung, "US Supreme Court poised to assess validity of key voting rights law," *Reuters*, August 1, 2025, 5:30 PM MDT. https://www.reuters.com/legal/government/us-supreme-court-poised-assess-validity-key-voting-rights-law-2025-08-01/

defend the right to vote for all citizens, and do not vote for politicians who have worked against voting rights. Let's keep the bar higher still. Early voting? Yes. Mail-in ballots? Yes. Expect county clerks to make voting easy. Expect representatives in state legislatures and the U.S. Congress to defend the Voting Rights Act and to bolster voter protections. Expect the U.S. Supreme Court to respect the Constitution and its Amendments, Congressional legislation, and judicial precedent.

Abolish Gerrymandering

On the issue of redistricting…you will have to trust me when I tell you that I started writing this manifesto in 2024, and I included gerrymandering in the centrist platform prior to the present furor that started in Texas, bled over into California, and is now spreading like a wildfire across the country.[46] I thought that I would be dragging the corpse of an absolutely boring political history lecture from the grave, something you last heard about in a high-school American Government class, and yet it has sprung out of the earth as a ravenous Kandarian zombie demon, alive in its undeath and searching anew for human flesh.

For readers who are not familiar, gerrymandering is the process of redrawing maps of voting districts to favor the political party that is presently in power in order to give

---

[46] The NPR Network, "The fight is on. How redistricting could unfold in 8 entangled states," *NPR*, August 14, 2025, 5:00 AM ET. https://www.npr.org/2025/08/14/nx-s1-5501537/texas-california-gerrymandering-redistricting

them an advantage in maintaining that power in upcoming elections.[47] It is a practice that all political parties have engaged in, when they have the power to do so and when they think they can get away with it. They often do it unapologetically, speaking publicly about gerrymandering as if it is part of the American tradition, a rightfully earned spoil of war. Yet, it is clearly against democracy and against the greater good. It creates a body of legislators that is not truly representative of the people, thus is diametrically opposed to the goals of our constitutional republic.

Gerrymandering brings the issue of morality front and center, and demands that we reflect on what it means to be a principled person and to do the right thing. Let's hear from the Father of the Nuclear Navy, known to be a hard-driving leader with a high bar for excellence and virtue:

> ...*morals and ethics are not relative; they do not depend on the situation. This may be the hardest principle to follow in working to achieve goals. The ends, no matter how worthy they appear, cannot justify just any means.*

— Admiral Hyman Rickover [48]

By this standard, it was immoral of Texas legislators to launch a gerrymandering campaign, and it was then also

---

[47] Michael Li, "Gerrymandering Explained," Brennan Center, August 9, 2025. https://www.brennancenter.org/our-work/research-reports/gerrymandering-explained

[48] Admiral Hyman Rickover, "Thoughts on Man's Purpose in Life," speech to the San Diego Rotary Club (1977). https://govleaders.org//rickover-purpose.php

wrong of Governor Gavin Newsom to fight fire with fire using Proposition 50 out of California in 2025.

I discussed this section of the manifesto with my dad as I was writing it, and I have to say that he does not agree. All throughout my childhood, my father was a self-employed, pull-yourself-up-by-your-bootstraps home builder. He ran his own construction business employing slightly shady laborers with names like *Neil O'Neil* and *Rick*. No last name, just *Rick*, like *Cher*, *Madonna,* or *Gandhi*. Actually, I believe that Neil and Rick were the same guy, just on different job sites. Whatever demons he may have had in his past, Rick was given a second chance to stand up and show his hard work ethic. My dad would sit down in his basement office for hours poring over blueprints of single family homes that he had designed, refining the details of utility room placement while listening to Rush Limbaugh on the AM radio. He would emerge periodically to find that we had stolen his drafting tape, brads, X-Acto knives, and Skilsaw in order to make battleships out of wood or Transformers out of cereal boxes. He might grumble, but he let us do it, as it was consistent with the number-one life lesson that he wanted to impart to us as kids.

It was only when I was an adult that Dad stated it explicitly, but his focus was always on self-reliance. You have to take the initiative to get things done in life. You need to use your common sense, experiment, and figure it out. You can't blame anyone else—it's up to you to do it. You need to take the duct tape by the horns. It's one of those things where I can see his message in hindsight, even if my ten-year-old self was not conscious of the lesson at the time.

My dad has been on a philosophical journey himself over the decades. He left Rush by the wayside long ago and moved toward the center, maybe even left of center. We certainly share a frustration with where things stand politically in America today, but his viewpoint now is that the Democrats need to take action. Proposition 50 in California is about self-reliance, in his view. It's pragmatic and is what's needed now to moderate the country.

When my kids were little and someone hit someone else in the eye, they would get a lecture from me about the cycle of violence. Retribution always leads to escalation, and so the cycle continues. It takes someone willing to stand for a higher principle to break the cycle. It's hard to do, to be sure. We fear that it shows weakness not to respond, but, in fact, it takes great strength to articulate the rationale for breaking the cycle and to bring the community along with you. This is thinking that applies to disagreements between kindergarteners as much as to nuclear deterrence and escalation theory. It applies to politics in the same way.

What about Akin's Eighth Law, you may ask? Beware of extreme positions. Wouldn't an absolute ban on gerrymandering be just that? I would argue that in our present redistricting arms race we have reached an extreme point, and that we need to push back toward a centrist posture that is good for the electorate.

So...I'm back to a Rickoverian *hard no* on partisan redistricting. This should be the common view of American centrists. If candidates know that independents will vote them out of office if they have participated in redistricting shennanigans, then they won't do it. But they have to know that they can't get away with it. We need independent centrists writing letters to Congress and making this point clearly. We need the middle to stand up for representative democracy. Thus, the centrist platform crucially includes zero tolerance for gerrymandering.

In fact, we must demand that Congress go a step further and enact legislation to provide protections against it. This is not new—these ideas are a part of the public debate already and include initiatives such as creating independent redistricting commissions.[49] In this approach, the people would elect members to a nonpartisan state commission that would follow the Voting Rights Act in drawing the map of voting districts for that state. It would make the process transparent and accountable to the citizens.

Another idea is to shift the American election system toward proportional representation, as is used in other democracies around the world.[50] It is hard to imagine this as being remotely possible in the present political climate, but it is worth considering for the future. There are different ways to implement proportional representation, but the essential idea is to move from a winner-take-all election system to an approach in which the number of

---

[49] Madeleine Greenberg, "How Can We Combat Gerrymandering?" *Campaign Legal Center*, August 7, 2025. https://campaignlegal.org/update/how-can-we-combat-gerrymandering

[50] Drew Penrose and Ansley Skipper, "How to end gerrymandering," *Protect Democracy*, August 20, 2025. https://protectdemocracy.org/work/how-to-end-gerrymandering/

representatives sent to Congress from each political party would be proportional to the way people voted. As pointed out in an explanatory video from *Vox*,[51] there is a block of New England states in which the vote is typically 30% Republican, and yet zero Republicans are sent to Congress. There are cases like this across the country, and it is fundamentally the result of the winner-take-all election system, made even worse through gerrymandering.

A pragmatic and stepwise approach may be advisable to eliminate the scourge of partisan redistricting. First, let's shift the dialogue from a struggle between left and right to a struggle for the center. Let's make gerrymandering akin to the nuclear taboo so that a politician wouldn't touch it with a ten foot pole. This will take voices from the middle. Second, let's pursue independent redistricting commissions, as Governor Schwarzenegger has done in California.[52] He's on the same page regarding an *absolute no* on gerrymandering, by the way. Think global, act local. We can push for independent redistricting commissions at the state level in addition to nationally. Eventually, once the tone has shifted sufficiently in the country, we can discuss proportional representation. You have to eat the elephant one bite at a time.

---

[51] Adam Freelander *et al.*, "Why US elections only give you two choices," *Vox*, YouTube (2024).
https://www.youtube.com/watch?v=bqWwV3xk9Qk&t=547s

[52] Melanie Mason, "Schwarzenegger tees off on Newsom's redistricting measure as 'insane,'" *Politico*, September 15, 2025. https://www.politico.com/news/2025/09/15/schwarzenegger-tees-off-on-newsoms-redistricting-measure-as-insane-00564813

Require Open Primaries

...That's Don Cunningham. He's the president and CEO of the Lehigh Valley Development Corporation, and he became mayor - just 31-years-old then - just after the Bethlehem plant stopped making steel.

People say - used to say all politics is local, remember that? People used to say all...

<u>Don Cunningham</u>: It's all national now. Unfortunately, like, the work that we've done here to revitalize this area...

<u>Michel Martin</u>: Yeah.

<u>Cunningham</u>: ...quite honestly, didn't involve presidents. It was us. You know, it went on for 20-plus years. Democrats, Republicans came and went from the White House, and we kept our head down and did what we needed to do.

<u>Martin</u>: Do you think you could get elected today?

<u>Cunningham</u>: I don't think so.

<u>Martin</u>: How come?

<u>Cunningham</u>: I'm not ideological enough for today. I probably couldn't get through a primary.

— Michel Martin interviewing Don Cunningham[53]

---

[53] Michel Martin and Steve Inskeep, "All Things Considered," *NPR*, 6:05 PM ET, October 22, 2024. https://www.npr.org/2024/10/22/nx-s1-5160699/morning-edition-hosts-share-their-election-reporting-from-pennsylvania

When you vote, it may sometimes feel that you don't have a lot of good choices. Often it is only two. And sometimes they suck, especially if you are an independent voter in a state with closed primaries. Why do they suck, you ask? It's because America's winner-take-all election system led very early on to the polarization into two dominant parties due to a natural concentration of power.[54] Why vote for a minority party when you know that one of the two dominant parties will end up winning? It seems more strategic to align your vote with the pole you like the best...or dislike the least. It's an arrangement that the Democratic and Republican parties don't comment on, but you know that they wouldn't have it any other way.

Once that psychology was entrenched, then third parties were essentially sidelined, and all the wringing of hands over issues and platforms moved internal to the parties as part of the primary election cycle. The primaries determine which party candidate will advance to the general election.

If you are an independent in a closed-primary state, then you miss this entire dialogue and chance to help shape the issues within the political parties. What's worse, the candidates have to win the support from their base, and, if it is a closed primary, then they will be more biased toward the left or toward the right. The end result is a general election featuring two extreme candidates...who suck

---

[54] Sarah Pruitt, "Why Does the US Have a Two-Party System?" *HISTORY*, May 27, 2025. https://www.history.com/articles/two-party-system-american-politics

swamp water. What's even worse still is that you are paying for it, since states support the cost of primary elections.

The solution? All states should have open primaries in which independent voters (those not registered with a political party) can vote for a member of any party in the primary elections, or can choose one party's ballot on which to vote in the primary. Any implementation of an open primary system would force the candidates away from the extremes and toward the center, knowing that more moderate voters will also be participating in the decision on who will advance to the general election. We would get away from candidates speaking to the extremes in the primary, then trying to back-pedal in the general election to seem more centrist. Do you really know how they will behave once elected?

This idea also is not new. Organizations such as Open Primaries[55] are advocating for this shift today so that the influence of the center would start at the beginning of the election cycle. What's even better is that this is both a local and a national issue. You can choose to vote for state and federal officials who support open primaries.

The political parties have disfavored open primaries in the past, arguing that independents have no business in the internal workings of their party.[56] I cannot agree with this.

---

[55] Open Primaries, https://openprimaries.org/
[56] Ashley Lopez, "The U.S. has a 'primary problem,' say advocates who call for new election systems," *NPR*, September 18, 2023, 5:00 AM ET.

If the public is funding the election, then all members of the public have the right to participate. A political party has no right to curtail democracy in their own interest.

So…that's it. Three points in the centrist platform, all aimed squarely at changing the architecture of American politics to reduce partisanship. I also considered other topics, such as campaign finance reform, rank choice voting, and the national popular vote versus the Electoral College. These are more complex and bear further study, but let's keep it simple. Let's push with passionate intensity for our country to take three small steps forward. If all Americans can vote for politicians who actually represent their district and who speak to the center, then we will have taken a giant leap toward supporting the greater good. If we can't break the cycle of violence against voting, redistricting, and representation in America, then we will continue to slide on the downward spiral toward democracy's demise and the state of barbarism that awaits at the bottom.

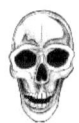

---

https://www.npr.org/2023/09/18/1199318220/nonpartisan-open-primaries-explainer

Case Studies

The world is changing. I see it in the streaming. I feel it in in the postings. I smell it in the airwaves.[57] Our minds are scattered and often fractured with the rush of social upheaval that has marked the first quarter of this century. We are so fragmented and distracted that we often forget to think critically. And our tribes have been chosen. Our emotions are now fixed, opinions settling into rutted troughs, ploughed decades ago, as a defense against the chaotic and ceaseless gale of data intertwined with rumor. Dinner conversation that turns to politics quickly sours the wine and spoils the food's flavor. Neighbors avoid eye contact, preferring the impersonality of tattered yard signs to the discomfort of discordant dialogue. Our bottled anger and frustration flows in spurts through tiny screens, resonating in echo chambers or else stagnating against unfriendly threats of cancellation.

Is this what we want? I can't think of anyone I know who is really happy with the state of society at present. We all feel that we have lost something, that there is a hollow place inside. We are missing something, and we are vulnerable to demagogues' and extremist shysters' attempts to sells us a replacement. But how can we actually find what's missing? And how can we get it back?

---

[57]   Yes, this is adapted from J. R. R. Tolkien, *The Lord of the Rings: The Return of the King*, George Allen and Unwin, London (1955).

We have to start with listening and thinking. Look again at the list of *Questions to Challenge your Perspective*. We must seek to understand the viewpoints of others and find common ground. We must pursue compromise so that we can implement pragmatic solutions to these tough issues and spend our energy instead on other pressing problems.

In this section of the manifesto, as an illustration, I will tackle a few of the thorniest political issues that have sown worsening division in America for at least half a century. I will draw some personal conclusions, but the main point here is not the opinions presented but rather the process used to consider the political spectrum. I will attempt to capture essential elements of what we all hope for and what we fear. You may disagree with my conclusions. That is just fine, but you can repeat the process for yourself, consider alternate views, weigh the greater good, and be prepared for a cogent and empathetic conversation with someone whose political leaning differs from your own. And you can have that conversation while making eye contact, enjoying a beer (or a Caprisun), and remaining friends. This is about the process of pursuing a punishing analysis of a polarizing issue while maintaining civility and respect for the people around you. It is about facing and rejecting fear, and behaving like a human.

I mentioned earlier the Polarity Management model of Dr. Barry Johnson.[33] In his book, Dr. Johnson develops a tool, which he calls the Polarity Map™, for graphically thinking through diametrically opposed viewpoints and charting a path that preserves the upsides of each perspective while avoiding the worst outcomes that each side dreads. I will

adapt and simplify his approach here and lay out what I
will call a Johnson-Cunningham matrix for these issues.
Yet again, I am not referring to Don Cunningham, former
mayor and CEO from the Lehigh Valley in Pennsylvania.
Rather, I am referring to the fictional Jim Cunningham, the
tragically-flawed motivational speaker from the movie
Donnie Darko[10] whose simplistic *Fear-Love* emotional scale
may yet bear more fruit. There is more to consider than I
include here...affordability, national debt, immigration...
this just opens the discussion. Let's jump into it.

Firearms

Columbine. The right of the people to keep and bear arms
shall not be infringed. Pulse. Vegas. Guns don't kill
people, people do. Sandy Hook. Parkland. Uvalde.

I realize, of course, that I am showing you my bias just by
the way I am introducing this topic. It's painful even to say
those names. Each time a school shooting is in the news,
I feel the brief rush of fear and my mind goes immediately
to my own kids. If you have kids, then you know what I
mean. You probably also know, deep in the pit of your
stomach, that something has to change.

But there is also the Constitution of the United States and
its first ten Amendments, known as the Bill of Rights,
which provide certain guarantees. I have argued for the
rule of law as a core principle of the American centrist, so
we must analyze this in detail. The language of the Second
Amendment is brief, and let's restate it here so that we can
be clear in our discussion.

Amendment II

A well regulated Militia, being necessary to the security of a free State, the right of the people to keep and bear Arms, shall not be infringed.[58]

Clearly, there have been changes in the use of the comma since the founding of our nation. Furthermore, there have been great changes in the nature of martial weaponry that we must consider. I mentioned Dr. Johnson's Polarity Management model as an inspiration for addressing tensions. Let's lay out a Johnson-Cunningham matrix for the politically unsolvable problem of firearms. On the horizontal axis, we state the viewpoints of the political left and the right. On the vertical axis is the Cunningham scale.

There is no question that this is an oversimplification. As Donnie Darko said,[10] it is incomplete to consider only fear and love as we deal with the complex space of human emotion. Likewise, only two columns, for *left* and *right*, cannot capture the full range of the political spectrum. Most situations are complex, with multiple poles competing for priority and resources. I will argue, though, that this is still a useful exercise. The more polarized America has become around an issue, the more applicable

58   The Bill of Rights: A Transcription, *The National Archives*. https://www.archives.gov/founding-docs/bill-of-rights-transcript

Firearms

	Pro Gun Control	Pro Gun Rights
Love	Peace is the norm Safe schools, kids, cities Concerns are respected Caring for the mentally ill	Full gun ownership rights Protect the Constitution Cultural preservation Preserve subsistence hunting as a way of life
Fear	School shootings Violent gun crime Bullied by the right Unsecured guns accessible to the mentally ill	Rights infringed Government overreach Tyranny from the left Disrespect of culture

is a bipolar model. At the very least, I hope this will offer some insight into understanding each other's perspectives.

What do we love? What do we fear? These things can define us. They can differentiate us, but I will argue that we are really not so different, and that we can find common ground even between disparate political orientations. As Dr. Johnson explains, our first goal in managing any polarity is to identify the positive state that each side seeks, and the negative outcomes that each side fears.[33] If we work together and are willing to compromise on a continuing basis, then we may be able to achieve much of the positive and avoid much of the negative. It will require iteration, keeping an open dialogue and being willing to course correct, but this ongoing process is itself the goal of the centrist in managing conflicting principles.

Please take a moment to read through the values that I have placed in the top row. This is my synopsis of what each side seeks. As you read through them, I would bet that you agree with most of these in both columns, whatever your political leaning. Look also at the bottom row. I similarly suspect that you will see validity with most of what is summarized there. The ire is raised and the listening stops when we try to implement an approach, and we allow disagreement to drive us back to rigid ideology. The devil is in the details, without question. But if we want real change, then we must be willing to work together, to keep listening, and to compromise. It's the only way to get things done.

Think for a minute about the person you trust most in this world. It could be a spouse, a parent, a sibling, or a friend. If the two of you had to work through a disagreement like this, you would do it while maintaining respect for them and seeking their respect. You would maintain your good relationship with them, since it is so foundational to getting along in the future. What if we thought of the country in this way, as a relationship and a trust that we needed to maintain?

I will keep in this mindset as I work through the Second Amendment, thinking about how to stay in the top row and avoid the bottom. Indulge me, if you will. Let's look at the language of the Constitution. It is so concise and simple that, arguably, it inadequately defines some of the terms and boundary conditions. So we will have to delve into that. Of key importance is the meaning of "infringe." Does it mean that we can pose absolutely no restrictions? Or does it mean that any restrictions implemented cannot fundamentally remove the ability to own and to bear arms?

What was the intent of the Second Amendment? The first phrase makes it clear that the Founders were concerned with the ability of the people to form a militia. What I learned in school, and I would guess you did as well, is that the primary concern was over a future emergence of a tyrannical government, and an armed populace would be able to stand up against a monarch or dictator to maintain the liberty of the people. I have also become aware in my adult life of an historical argument that the primary purpose of the Second Amendment was as a concession to Southern states who relied on militias to suppress slave rebellions, or more generally for state militias to suppress insurrections such as Shays' Rebellion.[59] Whichever view you find compelling does not really matter for the present discussion. The modern interpretation of this framing is that the intent was to preserve the right for the populace to own arms that were consistent with the state-of-the-art available to standing armies. The more commonly held view of the intent of the Second Amendment to deter and

---

[59] Carl T. Bogus, "The Hidden History of the Second Amendment (Winter 1998)," *U.C. Davis Law Review*, Vol. 31, p. 309 (1998). Roger Williams Univ. Legal Studies Paper No. 80. https://ssrn.com/abstract=1465114

to defeat an autocrat strengthens this interpretation, though it applies in either case.

The founders of our nation could not possibly have foreseen the march of technology into the atomic age, however. Alright, this next bit may sound a little crazy, but I told you that I am writing a manifesto, so it's got to have a little crazy in it. The Atomic Energy Act of 1954 opened up nuclear power to industry, but it also created the formal concept of classified material and defined the category known as Restricted Data related to nuclear weapons.[60] The U.S. Government asserted its authority and effectively drew a line: only the federal government may control nuclear weapon technology. There is no right for states to possess nuclear weapons. There is no right for corporations to develop nuclear weapons or their components, absent the delegated authority of the federal government. There is certainly no right for private citizens to own nuclear weapons. Not even tech billionaires.

To my knowledge, this prohibition has never been challenged. Certainly not seriously. Why? It should be as plain as the nose on your face. It is obviously an awful idea for individuals to own weapons of mass destruction. The probability that it would result in a catastrophic apocalypse of cataclysmic terror would be much too great. Free access

---

[60] U.S. Department of Energy, "Statutes, Regulations, and Directives for Classification Program," accessed October 2025. https://www.energy.gov/ehss/statutes-regulations-and-directives-classification-program

to nuclear weapons is clearly against the greater good, and so we do not allow it. To question *that* would be crazy.

So…we have established the principle that the federal government *can* forbid individual ownership of some form of arms. Then the question becomes: where do you draw the line? And is it a hard line, or a graded line with tighter controls on more dangerous weapons?

I'll return to my earlier assertion that the intent of the Second Amendment is to allow state militias to be armed commensurate with the weaponry routinely borne by soldiers in a standing army of the republic. This suggests that firearms up to the level of assault rifles, being the normal armament of a modern soldier, should be legal. Not every warfighter has access to an M1 Abrams, F-22 Raptor, or a W88 warhead, and it is appropriate to restrict private ownership of heavy munitions. There is no doubt that assault weapons are tremendously deadly, and a topic that draws great emotion, so I'll return to them shortly.

It remains to tackle what it means to "infringe" upon the right to bear arms. We have already stated that there is some line beyond which the government can outright ban possession of weapons for the sake of the greater good. Our definition of "infringe" should be correspondingly flexible in order to allow a reasonable, graded approach.

I will propose that if we interpret the Constitution as allowing a class of small arms to be owned legally by individual U.S. citizens, then we must have a clear process to initiate and maintain that ownership. But noninfringement is not the same as unfettered access. It cannot be, for the sake of the greater good. In my view, we are at present too far on the side of unfettered access to firearms in America.

We have all heard of gun show loopholes to procuring firearms, resistance to strengthening background checks, and mass shooters who obtained firearms through relatives. These are all extremely serious problems. We do not have nuclear weapon shows where you might go browse on a Sunday and pick up a B61. In fact, we have very stringent clearance procedures for federal employees and contractors who do any work pertaining to nuclear weapons technology. There are extremely strong protection requirements for both information and physical materials. The government and citizens working in the Nuclear Security Enterprise take these matters very seriously, and this is a very good thing.

Let's now consider data available from the U.S. Government on mass shootings. I began with a philosophical argument based on an interpretation of the Constitution, but any good policy that serves the greater good must be based on evidence.

This table is based on a research contract executed by Hamlin University for the U.S. Department of Justice and appears on the website of the National Institute of Justice.[61] The plots are based on fifty years of school shooting data compiled and analyzed by the Department of Homeland Security.[62] The statistics are troubling but offer insight.

A Half-Century of Mass Shootings[61]

98% of mass shooters were male
More than 69% of mass shooters were suicidal
63% had a history of violence
48% of mass shooters leaked their plans to others
77% used handguns; 25% used assault rifles
77% purchased at least some guns legally
80% stole guns from family members
80% of school shooters are under 21 years old[62]

[61] National Institute of Justice, "Public Mass Shootings: Database Amasses Details of a Half Century of U.S. Mass Shootings with Firearms, Generating Psychosocial Histories," February 3, 2022. https://nij.ojp.gov/topics/articles/public-mass-shootings-database-amasses-details-half-century-us-mass-shootings

[62] Based on analysis of the adjacent plots, attributed to the Center of Homeland Defense and Security of the Naval Postgraduate School, https://www.chds.us/c/; data obtained October 2025 from Statista at https://www.statista.com/statistics/971544/number-k-12-school-shootings-us-age-shooter/

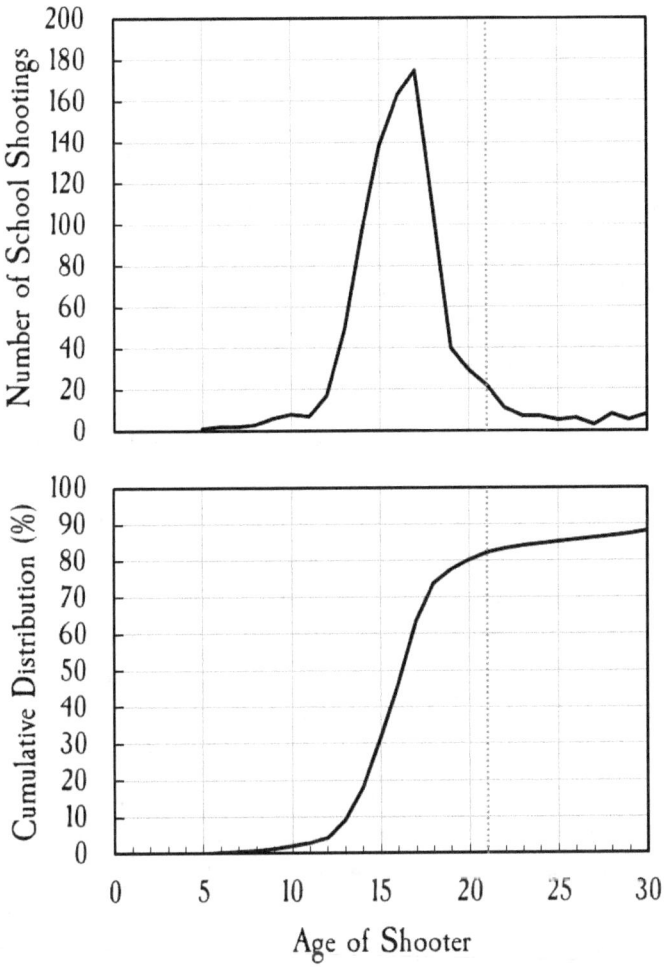

The fact that mass shooters are almost entirely men is known anecdotally but quantified strikingly here. The majority are in a state of mental crisis, have a violent history, and half reach out in advance to leak their plans. Is seems very plausible that these facts are a symptom of the broader mental health crisis being experienced by boys and men. Dr. Niobe Way calls it a "crisis of connection" in which our social norms and culture have created a sense of masculinity that discourages being in touch with our own emotions and building healthy emotional bonds with each other.[63] For some men and boys, lack of connection leads to isolation, which leads in turn to a sense of rejection. Dr. Way posits that, in the mind of a mass shooter, violence has become the solution that will put them on top of the social hierarchy. It is a tragic disconnect from reality and from their own humanity.

The fact that half of mass shooters leak information could then be a cry for help, but, in any case, it suggests a course of action, according to the National Institute of Justice analysis. "Red flag laws" should be implemented which would enable law enforcement to respond proactively to remove a firearm from the situation if friends and family report concerns that may be a precursor to a mass shooting. Universal background checks and a waiting period are also common sense measures—we certainly do these for security clearances, and it would be a modest price to pay to reduce gun violence. Legislation should be accompanied by a continued effort to build awareness of the "crisis of connection" and to change the culture experienced by men and boys.

---

[63]   Shannon Carpenter, "Boys and men are experiencing a 'crisis of connection,' expert says," *CNN*, July 17, 2024, 10:38 AM EDT. https://www.cnn.com/2024/07/17/health/boys-mental-health-niobe-way-wellness

The data in the table suggest other actions. Handguns, rather than assault weapons, are used in the majority of mass shootings, although incidents with assault weapons are typically 20% more deadly.[64] The majority of all of these weapons are either obtained legally or stolen from a family member or friend. Combine these statistics with the plotted distribution of the age of school shooters. The curve peaks at age 17, and indeed most of these shooters are young. Integrating the distribution in the top plot gives the cumulative distribution in the bottom plot, which reveals that 80% of school shooters are under age 21.

If we accept a national age limit of 21 for possession of all firearms, and make the legal and cultural changes to enforce this, we could then eliminate as many as 80% of these shootings. This means that we must construct a system in which sellers, including private sellers and vendors at gun shows, will not sell to underage individuals. We must also require gun safety devices such as trigger locks and gun safes. Gun owners and sellers must be held accountable to these standards, and this must become the cultural norm. This could also require an education campaign, federal or state subsidies for purchase of devices to secure guns, and possibly a voluntary gun buy-back program targeting assault weapons and handguns. We will have to get creative, and we must get serious.

---

[64]   Leslie M. Barnard *et al.*, "Firearm Type and Number of People Killed in Publicly Targeted Fatal Mass Shooting Events," *JAMA Netw. Open.* (2025). doi: 10.1001/jamanetworkopen.2024.58085; https://pmc.ncbi.nlm.nih.gov/articles/PMC11800013/

President Obama outlined a plan to reduce gun violence following Sandy Hook that contained many of these same thrusts.[65] All of them failed in Congress.[66] Why? There is a perdurable web of support for gun rights that links voters, representatives in government, and political groups.

Let me say a word about the National Rifle Association. The NRA dates back to 1871, founded with a focus on marksmanship rather than gun rights. It continues today to play a role in firearm use and safety classes that is altogether positive. But its absolutist position on gun rights is a problem. The NRA lobbies the federal and state governments and uses social engineering to fight actively against any legislation that would restrict gun ownership in any fashion. Since the 1977 pivot of the NRA to this extremist viewpoint and their ascension as a major political force on the national stage, the organization has consistently worked against any form of "common sense" gun legislation. It has weathered storm after storm of mass shootings—each time, the public mourning pushes sentiment toward gun legislation, and each time the NRA is a force in walking it back using fear tactics and carefully rehearsed talking points.[67]

---

[65] https://obamawhitehouse.archives.gov/node/193271

[66] Chris Cillizza, "The depressing lesson from 2013's failed gun control push," *CNN*, August 12, 2019, 4:35 PM EDT. https://www.cnn.com/2019/08/12/politics/congress-gun-laws-mcconnell

[67] Ron Elving, "The NRA Wasn't Always Against Gun Restrictions," *NPR*, October 10, 2017, 5:00 AM ET. https://www.npr.org/2017/10/10/556578593/the-nra-wasnt-always-against-gun-restrictions

This needs to change, but it can only change if there is a strong voice, that of the American center, demanding reasonableness. The NRA has its power only because it is granted to it by voters. There are some gun rights and gun control advocates whose opinions I will not change, but independent and moderate voters matter immensely here. You can vote for more centrist politicians and demand reasonableness, including in party primaries, where possible. Democrats can move to the middle and soften their demands for outright bans on firearms, while Republicans can reject the NRA report card and vote based on centrist principles and on a spirit of working together.

Gun rights hardliners fear that giving even an inch will start a cascade that will ultimately remove all Second Amendment rights. This is not the case. Common sense gun laws would make our nation stronger, and this is the spirit of compromise that needs to be at the heart of American centrism.

So, let me sum up my personal conclusions on the topic:

The American Centrist Firearms Checklist	
Total Ban on Assault Weapons	
Strong Universal Background Checks	✔
Waiting Periods and Red Flag Laws	✔
Age Limit (21) and Strong Enforcement with Gun Sellers	✔
Responsibility and Accountability for Securing Firearms	✔

You might disagree with the conclusions that I have drawn in this section. I certainly experienced pushback within my own family in not putting emphasis on an assault weapons ban, with one family member stating, "These are weapons of war, and we have shown as a human species that we are not capable of handling this technology. We can't have these things." I understand the sentiment, but, to me, the evidence points to the biggest lever being identifying boys in crisis early and keeping all guns out of their hands.

This is really not intended to be about my views, though. Rather, it is about the process of critical thinking and listening to opposing viewpoints. Look again at the Johnson-Cunningham matrix for firearms. Rewrite it yourself, if you prefer, and reframe some of the points. Think about the perspectives on each side. Think through what a compromise would look like that serves the greater good, one that realizes the upsides in both columns while avoiding the downsides. Use evidence to inform your decision. Then go vote. That's what this is about.

Abortion

Ok, another tough one. Maybe even tougher than firearms. For many people, the issue of abortion ties directly to their core values, religious or secular. Barring a complete change of outlook on life and social network, positions on abortion are nearly immutable. I am not going to change anyone's mind here—I have no illusions. But can we have a civilized discussion about such a polarizing issue? Taking a deep breath, let's attempt it.

Abortion

$\mathcal{P}$ro $\mathcal{C}$hoice	$\mathcal{P}$ro $\mathcal{L}$ife
Love	
Allow women to control their own life path	Protect the right to life of unborn humans
Protect women's rights over their bodies	Religious morals are respected
Uphold religious freedom	Support loving families
Fear	
Women's right to liberty and happiness curtailed	Violation of legal rights of unborn humans
Government overreach	Souls are damned
Tyranny from the right	Religion is disrespected
Breaking judicial precedent	Society grows immoral

Shown here is a Johnson-Cunningham matrix constructed this time for the issue of abortion, comparing values and fears of the pro-life and pro-choice perspectives. You may disagree with this framing—please rewrite it for yourself. This exercise is about the process of considering all sides and maintaining respect for those with different views.

We can see common ground within this matrix even as the stark contrast between the two viewpoints is evident. People on both sides value life, but there are several aspects of this to consider—the life of the unborn, the life of the mother, and the impact on the lives of her family on a decision in either direction. Both sides value religious freedom, to include freedom *from* religion for some; the liberty of the individual is clearly in tension with a sense of the greater good influenced by faith-based values. It is precisely because we all love freedom and life so much that this topic has become so politically charged.

In my mind, the issue comes down to how you define a human life. When does a collection of cells transition to become a human being? There is some line that we seek to draw that differentiates this, if imperfectly, that determines when the rights of a new human come into conflict with the freedoms of its mother.

The following table seeks to capture key milestones in the development of a human. You may research this further for yourself, but this was the most useful list that I was able to assemble to inform my own thinking. The first point to note is that the development of a human being is an extended process; the brain takes 25 years to mature fully. Medical science will not be able to point to a bright line and say, "Now you are human and deserving of rights." We will have to use judgement and accept ambiguity.

I mentioned earlier that I was raised Catholic, and I was pretty active through high school. When it came time to choose a patron saint, I picked St. George, the dragon slayer. He's an icon of the battle of good versus evil, and belies a pretty stark, black-and-white view of the Universe.

The Church's view on abortion is also black and white. Life begins at conception. Abortion is a hard no. You can't even use contraception (though I know some good-

Milestones in Human Development	
2 weeks	Conception creates a unique DNA sequence
6 weeks	Heart starts beating[68]
16-20 weeks	The Quickening—mother detects fetal movement[69]
18 weeks	Nerves formed allow pain signals to reach the brain[70]
24 weeks	Evidence that the brain responds to pain signals[70]
24 weeks	Viability—fetus may survive outside the uterus[71]
1 year old	Empathy—ability to comfort others in distress[72]
25 years old	Brain matures in planning and decision making[73]

[68] Jörg Männer, "When Does the Human Embryonic Heart Start Beating? A Review of Contemporary and Historical Sources of Knowledge about the Onset of Blood Circulation in Man," *J. Cardiovasc. Dev. Dis.*, June 2022. doi: 10.3390/jcdd9060187; https://pmc.ncbi.nlm.nih.gov/articles/PMC9225347/

[69] Cleveland Clinic, "Quickening in Pregnancy," April 22, 2022. https://my.clevelandclinic.org/health/symptoms/22829-quickening-in-pregnancy

[70] Royal College of Obstetricians and Gynaecologists, "Fetal Awareness: Review of Research and Recommendations for Practice" (2010). https://www.rcog.org.uk/media/xujjh2hj/rcogfetalawarenesswpr0610.pdf

[71] American College of Obstetricians & Gynecologists, "Facts Are Important: Understanding and Navigating Viability" (2025). https://www.acog.org/advocacy/facts-are-important/understanding-and-navigating-viability

[72] Jean Decety, "The Neurodevelopment of Empathy in Humans," *Dev. Neurosci.*, August 31, 2010. doi: 10.1159/000317771; https://pmc.ncbi.nlm.nih.gov/articles/PMC3021497/

[73] National Institutes of Health, "The Teen Brain: 7 Things to Know," Publication No. 23-MH-8078 (2023). https://www.nimh.nih.gov/health/publications/the-teen-brain-7-things-to-know

hearted American Catholics who may just quietly ignore that bit). The idea that a human soul is created at conception is common across many Christian denominations as well as other religions. This is not a scientific view, but there is perhaps a scientific analog that is worth mentioning. Conception creates a unique DNA sequence that has the potential to develop into a new human. Is that significant? Maybe. Maybe not.

DNA does seem almost miraculous—a double helix of proteins that contains all the information needed to create the body and mind of a human. It's either God at work in the world or an amazing example of emergent behavior in complex systems...or both. I would suggest that the potential is there, but the human is not yet. If you define human rights as beginning with DNA, then you are discounting the next miracle of the development of the human brain with the logic, emotion, passion, and personality that it will ultimately enable in a new person. Plus, you have created extremely difficult ethical questions for society in the area of medicine, including the practice of fertility treatments.

After the U.S. Supreme Court's Dobbs v. Jackson Women's Health Organization decision rolling back Roe v. Wade, the Alabama State Supreme Court ruled that fertilized embryos are humans. This immediately led to a crisis in the Republican party, as many Christians were users of *in vitro* fertilization in order to grow their families. As part of the IVF process, many fertilized embryos are created...and destroyed. Are we destroying humans or balls of cells? The end result is healthy babies for happy families. Again, we are faced with a question of whether the ends justify the means.

Following intense media coverage of IVF, many Republican politicians walked back their strong "life begins at conception" stance. Senator Josh Hawley, a Republican from Missouri and sponsor of the Life At Conception Act, rationalized it saying, "As a pro-life guy, I think that IVF is pro-life."[74] Then-Senator Marco Rubio said, "It's a balancing act that as a society we're going to have to make."[74] IVF created an ethical dilemma, a tension between principles, which drove many pro-lifers away from drawing a bright line at conception.

From a secular and political perspective—certainly from a logical perspective—I think this debate is over. Dobbs and IVF combined in ironic fashion to create a cognitive dissonance for the religious right. Even as many still say they agree that life begins at conception, 63% of white evangelical Protestants, higher fractions of other Christian groups, and 70% of American adults overall say that IVF is a good thing.[75] As a society, I believe we have decided that the full rights of an individual cannot begin absolutely

---

[74] Lexie Schapitl, "How IVF is complicating Republicans' abortion messaging," *NPR*, March 16, 2024, 5:00 AM ET. https://www.npr.org/2024/03/16/1238966404/how-ivf-is-complicating-republicans-abortion-messaging

[75] Gabriel Borelli, "Americans overwhelmingly say access to IVF is a good thing," *Pew Research Center*, May 13, 2024. https://www.pewresearch.org/short-reads/2024/05/13/americans-overwhelmingly-say-access-to-ivf-is-a-good-thing/

at conception, that DNA alone does not make the human, and we will have to keep looking further for the boundary between ball of cells and nascent citizen.

In only a handful of weeks after conception, a heartbeat can be detected in a human fetus. You've probably seen a billboard stating this fact, part of a push by the pro-life movement to build public support for banning abortion early in pregnancy. As of September 2025, twelve U.S. states have a total abortion ban, but another five have a six-week abortion ban,[76] products of a national campaign to institute state and federal "heartbeat" laws that seek to use the heart to define the beginning of human life and of rights for protection as an individual. Is there something to this? We may connect emotionally with a detectable heartbeat, but does it have true medical significance?

Many physicians argue no. Dr. Christina Han and Dr. Cara Heuser, experts in high-risk pregnancies, write that "a beating heart is neither a necessary nor sufficient standard to determine the start of life, making antiabortion heartbeat bills morally and legally wrong."[77] Their argument is that this is an arbitrary boundary not based on any medical information differentiating the development of a human.

---

[76] KFF, "Abortion in the United States Dashboard," September 2, 2025. https://www.kff.org/womens-health-policy/abortion-in-the-u-s-dashboard/

[77] Christina Han and Cara C. Heuser, "Antiabortion Heartbeat Bills Are neither Morally nor Legally Sound," *Scientific American,* January 23, 2023. https://www.scientificamerican.com/article/antiabortion-heartbeat-bills-are-neither-morally-nor-legally-sound/

The heart and circulatory system are not fully formed at the time that the first electrical impulses and muscle cell motion begins—this is a process that continues for weeks to come. Setting an arbitrary limit on medical procedures here removes ethical decisions from the hands of the woman arbitrarily and restricts the standard of care delivered by a physician.

Another arbitrary boundary is the detection of early fetal motion by the mother, known as *the quickening*. This was used in medieval times as a marker of the start of life, but has very little medical meeting in our modern understanding. A fetus begins moving around 12 weeks, though this is undetectable to the pregnant woman. A mother who has previously experienced pregnancy can sense the quickening as early as 16 weeks, though it is often not detectable until 20 weeks or later.[69] Definitions with ethical importance that rely on our detection capabilities, or on technology in any fashion, are not really based on solid principles.

Being human is less about muscle and more about mind. It's not about the heart, arms, legs, or kneecaps. It's our capacity for logic, empathy, language, story-telling, and all of the mental characteristics distinct from other animals that make us unique. So when does the mind become *human*? What is our goalpost? This may not be so easy to define. The brain continues to develop rapidly even in teenagers, and it is not until a person's mid-to-late twenties that the prefrontal cortex matures, along with abilities for planning, prioritization, and decision making.[73] The brain is certainly developing and changing all through childhood.

81

Key emotional functions such as empathy begin around one year old, when infants start to exhibit the behavior of comforting those in distress.[72] I certainly found it amazing and rewarding when my own kids started really smiling at mom and dad at just a few months of age. Newborn babies clearly feel distress and comfort, so emotions of a foundational form are there from birth. What are the developmental milestones of the brain *in utero*? When do we begin to feel and to think? When are we self-aware?

The best discussion on this that I found was a report reviewing research on fetal awareness by the Royal College of Obstetricians and Gynaecologists.[70] Significant attention in that report is given to when a fetus becomes sufficiently aware to feel pain. The authors point out that this cannot be possible before pain receptors, the nerves to transmit pain, and a brain capable of receiving and processing the signals are all present. Research has shown based on hormonal stress response that "information about tissue damage has reached the midbrain" starting at 18 weeks, however, at this stage, the brain may not interpret these signals as pain. By 24 weeks, however, synapses in the cortex have formed that may allow the brain to interpret sensory information, and, furthermore, "there is direct evidence of neural activity in the primary sensory cortex following tissue damage in very premature infants equivalent to 24 weeks of gestational age." In other words, there is pretty solid evidence that at 24 weeks, a fetus is fully capable of feeling pain.

This happens to correspond to the age of "viability," that is, the time at which a fetus can survive outside the womb.

There is actually a probability distribution for the survival of a baby outside the womb as a function of age, but 24 weeks is at the edge of the cliff.[71] For now. This is the problem with any definition of human rights based on technology. It is likely to be a moving target unmoored by common values or principles.

The concept of viability has been central to the abortion debate since it was used in Roe v. Wade to define the span of constitutional protections for abortion rights. Research groups today are developing artificial womb technologies which they hope will improve outcomes for premature births, but this would also shift the definition of viability much earlier.[78] Should we allow our sense of what it means to be human be affected by the state of technology?

If you have followed me this far and want to know what yet another man talking about abortion has to say, then I'll tell you. I resonate strongly with coupling a definition of the beginning of individual rights to the emotional development of the human mind. My personal conclusion is that the federal government should protect abortion rights up to 24 weeks based on brain development, not viability. Arguments to ban abortion prior to that point in human development are based on religious values, and the

---

[78]   Rob Stein, "An artificial womb could build a bridge to health for premature babies," *NPR*, April 12, 2024, 8:00 AM ET. https://www.npr.org/sections/health-shots/2024/04/12/1241895501/artificial-womb-premature-birth

First Amendment to the Constitution makes it clear that rule of law must be tied to secular values, not to religion.

While I understand that there are deep moral concerns for many people of faith, I would ask them to consider that there are conflicting values between their beliefs and the Constitutional rights of a woman over her own body. In challenging ethical situations, people need the freedom and the trust placed in them to make their own decisions. This is part of free will, and we must let free people be free. They are the ones most affected by their circumstances, and they will ultimately be the ones most affected by the consequences of a decision in either direction.

> *While people may have differing views on abortion, those views must not interfere with the relationship between people and their clinicians. People should be able to access the health care they need from the clinicians who understand their patients' situation and have patient health and well-being in mind.*

> — The American College of Obstetricians & Gynecologists[71]

I include this quote here as a reminder that many medical associations including the ACOG and the American Medical Association have advocated for abortion rights so that they can deliver a high standard of medical care. The present state of abortion law in our country, including enormous differences from state to state, is unstable, unsustainable, and untenable. Abortion restrictions and the threat of imprisonment to doctors is leading physicians in states like Texas to perform hysterectomies rather than standard abortions in order to avoid prosecution.[79] This is not serving the greater good. These procedures are riskier than abortions and result not only in the termination of the pregnancy, but in women no longer able to become pregnant in the future. There are numerous other stories of women being denied care while having a miscarriage, even while bleeding dangerously, in post-Dobbs America.

We are nowhere near an equilibrium when it comes to constructing abortion laws that aim for the greater good. You may disagree with my conclusions, but I see no solution other than a compromise implemented through federal legislation that will allow doctors to deliver quality care and to keep their Hippocratic oath to do no harm. We need a solution that follows the Constitution, performs the "balancing act" between rights which may be in conflict, and results in the emergence of common sense medical decisions by women, in consultation with their doctors, that benefit their own health and their family's well-being.

I have made a case for allowing women to make this decision without governmental restrictions prior to 24 weeks of pregnancy. This timeframe is not arbitrary nor technology-dependent, but is based on a modern medical understanding of human brain development. What about

---

[79]   Selena Simmons-Duffin, "Doctors who want to defy abortion laws say it's too risky," *NPR*, November 23, 2022, 5:01 AM ET. https://www.npr.org/sections/health-shots/2022/11/23/1137756183/doctors-who-want-to-defy-abortion-laws-say-its-too-risky

after 24 weeks? That is less obvious to me; my conclusion from the evidence is that there is then a conflict between the rights of the woman and those of the unborn. A compromise could leave this in the provenance of the states to decide. It is meaningful to note that fewer than 1% of abortions happen in the third trimester,[80] and surely this situation must involve extremely difficult discussions between the pregnant woman and her doctor.

The utilitarian lever arm here is in making a clear-eyed and evidence-based decision on abortion access prior to the extensive fetal brain development that happens in the final trimester. It was a journey for me to arrive at this place in my thinking—for many years I invoked the uniqueness of DNA to remove cognitive dissonance between religious and secular values. But meditate for yourself on this question, whose answer, informed by evidence, should point the way forward to a national reconciliation on the topic of abortion. Change the word *human* to *sentient*, and this question may also apply to AI ethics before too long.

The Key Question on Life and Freedom

What does it mean to be human and thus to have rights?

---

[80] Katrina Kimport, "Less than 1% of abortions take place in the third trimester – here's why people get them," *The Conversation*, May 17, 2022 8:24am EDT. https://theconversation.com/less-than-1-of-abortions-take-place-in-the-third-trimester-heres-why-people-get-them-182580

Transgender

I must not fear.
Fear is the mind-killer.
Fear is the little-death that brings total obliteration.
I will face my fear.
I will permit it to pass over me and through me.
And when it has gone past, I will turn the inner eye to see its path.
Where the fear has gone there will be nothing. Only I will remain.

— The Bene Gesserit Litany Against Fear
from *Dune* by Frank Herbert[8]

This section on case studies in centrism is proving to be the most demanding part of writing this *Moderate Manifesto*. I am repeatedly compelled to do more research, to question my own thinking, and to clarify my own values, which are often in wicked tension. This is a good exercise in self-examination and in self-awareness. I recommend that you repeat the process for yourself, especially if you disagree with my conclusions.

Alright, so why did I start a discussion on transgender people with the Litany? You may have already guessed. If not, then I'll tell you in a minute. First, let's construct the Johnson-Cunningham matrix, and let's go beyond just transgender to capture trends in the thinking on LGBTQ+ issues of those in the general population on the left and of those on the right. What do we love, and what do we fear? This is another topic that has been in the news *ad nauseam* lately so we will have much material to draw from.

LGBTQ+

	Modern Allies	Traditional Values
Love	Allow humans to control their own life path Love and respect all people Equal opportunity for all	Preserve the sacred institution of marriage Support loving families Ensure fairness for girls
Fear	Prejudice curtails rights and opportunities Disrespect harms mental health, increases suicides Government overreach	Society grows immoral Violation of religious norms and freedoms Fairness violated by the left

There has been enormous change in attitudes toward homosexuality in the last several decades. We went from coming out of the closet being the kiss of death for most careers, through the awkward "don't-ask-don't-tell" era, to the place we are at today, where, in most professional circles, being gay is no big deal. You might be a redhead, you might be Hispanic, you might be gay—let's work together and get the job done. That's how it should be.

The legalization of same-sex marriage in the landmark case Obergefell v. Hodges was a watershed moment in this country. In 2015, the Supreme Court ruled that marriage between two people regardless of gender must be guaranteed nationally given the Constitutional rights of due process and equal protection.[81] This was a big deal for gay couples. Not only was it a public recognition of the legitimacy of their civil unions, but it had extremely pragmatic consequences regarding things such as coverage on health insurance and inheritance of a partner's estate, allowing a survivor to remain in their home. Fast forward to today, and 70% of Americans now support same-sex marriage as being legally recognized.[81] I view this as a settled societal matter. All people are entitled to life, liberty, and the pursuit of happiness, and the ability to marry is a practical necessity to realize this self-determined path and to function as a household in our society.

But LGBTQ+ issues are still controversial and still in the news. The present hot-button topic is transgender persons, gender identity, and trans rights held in tension with traditional values regarding gender. Trans girls in sports became a highly polarized issue during the 2024 election, and I'm sure we all saw images on the news that quickly divided the nation into camps either supporting trans athletes or calling for "no boys in girls' sports."[82]

---

[81] Julie Carr Smyth, *The Associated Press*, "What to know about the Supreme Court ruling that legalized same-sex marriage 10 years ago," *PBS*, June 26, 2025, 2:55 PM EDT.
https://www.pbs.org/newshour/politics/what-to-know-about-the-supreme-court-ruling-that-legalized-same-sex-marriage-10-years-ago

[82] *The Associated Press*, "Trans athlete wins two girls events at California track and field finals," *NBC News*, June 2, 2025, 9:07 AM MDT. https://www.nbcnews.com/nbc-out/out-news/trans-athlete-wins-two-girls-events-california-track-field-finals-rcna210386

I will tell you that I felt uneasy about this whole issue as it was unfolding. There are fairness issues both for trans athletes and for cisgender girls in sports; I have tried to capture these conflicted views in the Johnson-Cunningham matrix. Again, there is common ground to be seen even in the midst of the conflict. We all want our young people to have opportunity. We want them to be loved and to be treated fairly. We want them to meet their potential. It seems to me that there is some aspect of the situation that I could not quite figure out, though. To think through it now, let's start by hunting for relevant evidence.

There is a very thoughtful report and fact sheet produced jointly by the nonpartisan health policy organization KFF and by *The Washington Post* in 2023.[83] Key findings from that study, along with one from a 2025 AP-NORC poll,[82] are included in the following table. The study paints a fairly bleak picture of what it is like to be a transgender person in America today. Trans individuals suffer high rates of mental health issues, have trouble accessing health care, report high levels of discrimination in career pursuits, and are verbally and sometimes physically attacked due to their gender identity. Their feelings of hope and happiness are lower than average, while depression and loneliness are greater. While the focus in the news has been on trans female athletes, it is worth noting that the majority of transgender Americans do not identify as a man or as a woman but are gender-nonconforming or nonbinary.[83]

---

[83] Ashley Kirzinger *et al.,* "KFF/The Washington Post Trans Survey," *KFF*, March 24, 2023. https://www.kff.org/mental-health/poll-finding/kff-the-washington-post-trans-survey/

Transgender in America [83]
Less than 1% of American adults are transgender
66% realized they were trans in childhood
78% felt more satisfied with life after transitioning
63% feel discriminated against due to being trans
43% have had suicidal thoughts in the last year
70% of Americans adults think trans female athletes should not be allowed in girls sports [82]
54% think the mental health of trans girls will suffer if they are not allowed in girls' sports

The issues around LGBTQ+ identities are more complex than you would glean from typical sports-focused treatment in the mainstream media, which arguably has not reported adequately on the full situation. Is the issue of trans athletes in girls' sports a big problem? Is it worthy of national news? Should we let it divide us?

I'll reiterate that less than 1% of Americans identify as transgender, and out of that group only a small percentage again are interested in playing competitive school sports. Prior to changing the rules in 2025 to bar trans women from collegiate female sports, the NCAA stated that there are fewer than 10 transgender women playing college sports nationally.[84] In my own state of New Mexico, a group of legislators sponsored a bill that would have banned trans athletes from women's sports; it was defeated following contentious debate. Proponents cited injuries to cisgender girls by trans athletes and fairness issues, but could not point to any instances of current trans athletes in our state between middle school and college age, let alone any injustices that had occurred here. Referring to the stories told regarding the negative impact of trans athletes on cisgender girls, State Representative Liz Thomson said, "the plural of anecdote is not data."[84]

Let me now tell you my opinion on this seemingly thorny issue. The transgender controversy is a red herring. It is not worthy of national news in the way that is happening today. Less than 10 collegiate trans athletes? I'm sorry but this is just not the most pressing issue for the nation. It is receiving so much publicity as it is being pushed by populist elements on the political right as a wedge issue. It is being used explicitly to divide people so as to isolate and consolidate political support. This is why I started with the Litany Against Fear—we need to see it and name it when society is being shoved to the bottom of the Herbert-Maslow hierarchy. In addition to both our trans and cisgender kids, the other victims of this behavior are national unity, the greater good, and democracy.

---

[84]   Nash Jones, "NM bill to bar trans women from women's sports effectively defeated," *KUNM,* February 13, 2025, 7:47 PM MST. https://www.kunm.org/local-news/2025-02-13/nm-bill-to-bar-trans-women-from-womens-sports-effectively-defeated

I was upset enough by the tone of our state's debate that I wrote a letter to my own Republican state representatives and to Representative Thomson:

I am an independent voter and one of your constituents. I have typically voted conservative in state elections as I find it valuable to have fiscally conservative voices in state government to control spending and ensure a balanced budget. I may change this approach in the future due to my deep disappointment with the direction of national politics and the fact that this is starting to have local effects in New Mexico.

I was disappointed to see anti-trans legislation come before the New Mexico legislature. This is a total distraction to the important work that needs to happen in the state, and in my view is a fear-based tactic to win support... If you value the votes of fiscally-conservative independents in your district, then you will not allow this to happen again. Focus on governing New Mexico and not on highly politicized and bogus ideology targeting minority populations. I am copying Representative Liz Thomson on this email to thank her for her articulation that "the plural of anecdote is not data" and for keeping attention on making decisions based on real data and evidence, and focusing on real issues. That is the leadership that I would like to see within the New Mexico legislature regarding effective governance...

Please do your work with reasonableness in mind, and with the greater good of the state of New Mexico and the nation in your hearts.

Comparatively few cisgender girls are impacted by the presence of trans athletes, but I absolutely do acknowledge that there is a fairness issue here that needs to be addressed. Per the KFF/*Washington Post* study, most Americans see that disallowing trans girls from participating in sports will hurt their mental health. We are torn here, I think. We sense unfairness on both sides of the issue. What's the solution? With numbers so small, I don't think that there can be one uniform approach. I would suggest that the best solutions will be local. Sports in public schools are publicly funded, and trans kids have a right to access them.

A school principle could approach this issue with compassion. I'll tell you how I would do it. It would require many discussions with parents, with coaches, with students, with school administrators, perhaps with legislators, mayors, or governors. First of all, I would seek clarity on the state law and on district policy, as we follow the rule of law. I would ensure the stakeholders understood the principles that we are holding in tension around fairness, liberty, and taxpayer rights. When I had earned the trust of students, parents, and school administrators that I would be fair, I would then propose a range of solutions, from full participation in girls' sports, practice but not playing in games, playing with the boys' teams...we would lay it out and talk through the plusses and minuses. This would take time and effort, but anything done well takes time and effort. We would also circle back at the end of the season for listening sessions to collect feedback on how it went. And I would do the same thing for a trans boy who wanted to participate in boys' sports. (Why are they never in the news, by the way?)

Throughout, I would work hard to value the perspectives of all involved. It does not make you a bad person to have feelings in one way or the other on this. On the *Hidden Brain* podcast, Professor Dannagal Young offered insight:[85]

> ...*Need for closure is associated with more negative opinions of transgender people, transgender candidates, and transgender rights. And this is one of those things that is intuitive on its face. And when we thought about studying this construct, I just thought, you know, for folks who need for there to be a yes or no answer, black and white, it would make sense for these folks, the concept of gender fluidity or the concept of gender being a social construct, that I could imagine that that might be hard for them to reconcile. And sure enough, our results actually showed quite a robust effect of need for closure on these outcomes... A society that only has people who are tolerant of ambiguity and high in need for cognition, well, it might be a society that has art and music and innovation, but it might also be a society that could be attacked and taken over very quickly... A society that only has high need for closure and low need for cognition, that is a society that might be super safe, super high in law and order, but might not have the kind of innovations and exploration, art and culture that would make quality of life really rich. So thinking about these two things as the yin and the yang of society, rather than things that need to be demonized...I think is necessary.*

---

[85] *Hidden Brain* staff, "Sitting with Uncertainty," September 30, 2024. https://hiddenbrain.org/podcast/sitting-with-uncertainty/

We need everyone. We need all of the opinions, all of the worries, all of the energy, all of the passionate intensity. We need to be working together and finding common ground. This is what makes our country great. We cannot allow discomfort with transgender identities to be a wedge issue. We were in that space with gay rights decades ago, and we moved forward. From the perspective of the American centrist, we must respect others, and we must recognize the LGBTQ+ community as a minority that cannot be allowed to suffer from a tyranny of the majority. Let free people be free.

One of my kids has a nonconforming gender identity. If I have some passion around this issue myself, then this is why. But it was a difficult journey. It started in high school—different haircuts, other signs of what I thought was your typical subversion of the patriarchy. Like most adults of my generation, I had a very negative reaction when the request came to use *they/them* pronouns. "*So you are telling me that I have to carry the mental load of remembering to refer to you differently than I have throughout your entire life? It's not even correct grammar. Why is that a fair request?*" We went back and forth on these things, struggled with explaining it to the grandparents who said, "*Oh, it's just a phase,*" but at the end of the day I realized something. Here is my kid, who I have loved since they were a baby just learning to smile at mom and dad. Here is my kid, becoming more self-aware and moving toward independence, and they are asking me to recognize them. They are asking me to love them still. And I had to decide to reboot my perspective and start with "I love you" and then focus on the important things. Does it matter if they wear a halter top or a button-up shirt, stretch pants or long overalls? No, it does not. What matters is that they have a good friend group, that they get along with their siblings, that they study hard in school, go to college, and develop a career plan. It matters whether they try to help others and are kind, whether they try to make a positive difference in the world.

The Centre for Heterodox Social Science, a right-leaning group at the University of Buckingham which seeks to present evidence-based counterpoints to more liberally-biased academic research, has studied transgender identity. They present research data indicating that the number of young people identifying as transgender has decreased significantly from 2023 to 2025.[86] Fox News has highlighted data from the CHSS report (while omitting some of the data that did not support their narrative) and suggested that youth are realizing that their identification as nonbinary was in error and then detransitioning.[87] My judgement is that the CHSS data cited are valid, but I reserve judgement on the interpretation. I wonder if the present political climate has any impact on willingness to identify or to express an identity as transgender. But here's a key point: *This does not change anything that I have said above.*

---

[86] Eric Kaufmann, "CHSS Report No. 5: The Decline of Trans and Queer Identity among Young Americans," The Centre for Heterodox Social Science, University of Buckingham (2025). https://www.heterodoxcentre.com/research/chss-report-no-5/

[87] Fox & Friends Weekend, "Report finds fewer students identifying as nonbinary amid debate over child gender surgeries," *Fox News Channel*, October 18, 2025. https://www.foxnews.com/video/6382933432112

It is possible that, for some kids, it is in fact a phase or an experiment as they seek to define themselves in adolescence. Parents should still talk to them with a seek-to-understand attitude. Ask them how they are feeling and why. These kids deserve the respect and kindness of society. They deserve for their families to love them just as much as when they were a baby smiling for the first time.

I'll end this section with a remarkable quote from one of the founding fathers of utilitarianism. We sometimes think that the world is changing only now…but it has actually been evolving for quite some time.

> *The entire history of social improvement has been a series of transitions, by which one custom or institution after another, from being a supposed primary necessity of social existence, has passed into the rank of a universally stigmatised injustice and tyranny. So it has been with the distinctions of slaves and freemen, nobles and serfs, patricians and plebeians; and so it will be, and in part already is, with the aristocracies of colour, race, and sex.*

— John Stuart Mill, 1863[88]

---

[88] John Stuart Mill, "Chapter 5: On The Connexion Between Justice And Utility," *Utilitarianism*, (1863).
https://utilitarianism.net/utilitarian-quotes/

A False Polarity

> *I don't understand how in a country of 200 million voters, we only have two political parties. We have eight kinds of Coke, but only two political parties.*

— Jon Stewart[89]

You may have followed me through the centrist case studies and thought that I was biased toward a progressive viewpoint. After all, I argued to protect abortion rights through the first half of pregnancy, regulate gun ownership, and protect trans rights. Unless you are on the left of the political spectrum yourself, in which case you may be upset with me. After all, I argued that states should be able to ban abortion in the second half of pregnancy, that assault weapons should be legal, and that trans rights might not extend to playing in women's sports. Here's the problem with all of this: *Why are left and right the only options?*

Just as Donnie Darko argued that the Cunningham scale, running from *fear* to *love*, was too simplistic to capture the full range of human emotions, I would also argue that *left* to *right* is too constraining for considering political opinion

---

[89] Jon Stewart, *The Daily Show*, *Comedy Central*, August 16, 2000. https://thinkmindful.com/eight-kinds-of-coke-jon-stewart/ https://www.reddit.com/r/quotes/comments/4z8vfo/im_anti_political_parties_i_dont_understand_how/

and formulating policy. Yet, we have allowed this to become engrained in our collective American psyche.

This one-dimensional thinking is reinforced by our winner-take-all political system, as discussed earlier, and routinely treated as the norm by news media. How often do we hear politicians or political camps characterized as right or left, conservative or progressive, Republican or Democrat? It's a constant thread throughout the daily news cycle, and society in general is largely incapable of articulating the notion that there is an alternative axis, or even a centrist position on issues. Lately, we hear, "Oh, the Republicans are doing this now, and we are waiting for the Democrats to respond." Where is the voice of the center? The nearly complete exclusion of voices other than Democrat or Republican is a false dichotomy. It is the very definition of the limited "either/or thinking" discussed by Dr. Barry Johnson in his Polarity Management model.[33] I have referenced this model in developing the case studies of challenging political issues that we have discussed previously, but it is time to take a clue from Donnie Darko and to expand beyond a false political polarity.

The present state of American politics looks like this:

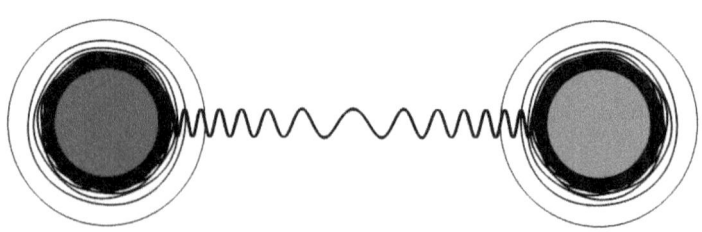

What if we changed the structure of American politics and civil society so that it looked like this?

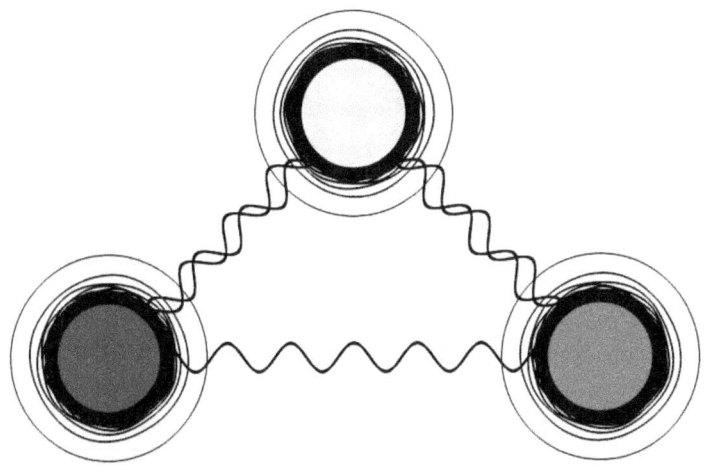

You do not have to choose between the Democratic and Republican parties. You can be *independent*. You can think through each choice during an election and vote your conscience. If your state has open primaries, you can even help to push the parties toward the center. When I look at my voter registration information on our state's website, it says *NO PARTY / DECLINED TO SELECT*. I'm pretty happy with that right now, at this moment in history.

As the graphic suggests, we perhaps should not even think of centrism as sitting on the same axis as the two dominant political parties. The Centrist Decoder Ring (shown at the start of the book) could become a map, with the left-right axis going from progressive to conservative, and the vertical axis from autocracy to democracy. The voice of the American centrist could pull up the entire political spectrum, Democrats, Republicans, and third parties, toward a place of greater democratic stability, functionality, and harmony in political discourse.

George Washington himself issued a warning against political parties in his Farewell Address to the nation, delivered upon completing his second term in office:[90]

The alternate domination of one faction over another, sharpened by the spirit of revenge natural to party dissension, which in different ages and countries has perpetrated the most horrid enormities, is itself a frightful despotism. ... It serves always to distract the public councils and enfeeble the public administration. It agitates the community with ill founded jealousies and false alarms, kindles the animosity of one part against another, foments occasionally riot and insurrection.

Sound familiar? Political parties are inevitable, particularly in a winner-take-all political system. You can't blame politicians for joining them, as it is a rare individual who can win an election as an independent. Angus King, Joe Lieberman, Bernie Sanders...Dan Osborn came close.[91] But as a voter, you cannot put your faith in political parties.

---

[90] George Washington, "Farewell Address," *Daily American Advertiser,* Philadelphia, September 19, 1796.
https://www.senate.gov/artandhistory/history/resources/pdf/Washingtons_Farewell_Address.pdf

[91] Michael A. Cohen, "How an independent candidate put Nebraska Republicans on the ropes," *MSNBC,* Nov. 5, 2024, 4:00 AM MST. https://www.msnbc.com/opinion/msnbc-opinion/senate-election-nebraska-osborn-fischer-rcna178232

Why is it that those who seek power tend to gain it? It is natural selection. A politician who is not self-promoting and who is not willing to bend their principles in order to gain power is at an extreme disadvantage relative to those who will do what it takes to win. This is an unfortunate truth of Nature and competition between human animals.

The same is true of political parties. A party does not survive and dominate national politics unless it has the cultural aspects of self-preservation and the desire for power. Thus, any dominant political party fundamentally does not have your interest in mind, nor the best interest of the nation. The priorities are winning and survival in order to fight and win another day. Your duty as a voter is to see through these tendencies and to discern which candidate, *despite* their party affiliation, is more genuinely focused on service and the good of the nation.

There are some groups already that embrace a dialogue between the left and the right, including the Braver Angels, who aim to "bridge the partisan divide and strengthen our democratic republic."[92] They host events and facilitate one-on-one conversations between people of opposing views, encouraging them to see the humanity in each other. My only challenge to these efforts is this: Let's not bridge the divide, let's fill that chasm with American centrism.

---

[92]   https://braverangels.org/

The Riddle of Steel

Yes! You know what it is, don't you, boy? Shall I tell you?
It's the least I can do. Steel isn't strong, boy, flesh is stronger!
… That is strength, boy! That is power!
What is steel compared to the hand that wields it?

— Thulsa Doom from *Conan the Barbarian*[5]

This moderate manifesto is not about Donald Trump. In fact, I haven't even mentioned him up until this point (Okay, maybe his name appeared in one footnote in the book.) But here is one thing that I will say: It was a mistake for Kamala Harris to name Donald Trump as weak during the 2024 election cycle.

Love him as a champion of the people or hate him as an authoritarian demagogue, there is no denying that Trump understands the riddle of steel. In its essence, the riddle is a statement on the power of the people. In the last decade, Trump has reshaped the G.O.P., moving the party of Lincoln along its arc from preservation of the union, through patriotic conservatism, to a new focus on…well… power. He did this through his remarkable charisma, confidence, and persuasiveness. He did this by identifying with working-class Americans, understanding their hopes and their fears, and motivating them to vote. There is no name for that other than *strength*. When Harris called it otherwise, it rang hollow with many Americans and weakened her own hand.

Donald Trump's name was never mentioned at the funeral of Senator John McCain.[93] Three ex-presidents and many other servants of the nation attended the gathering for the long-time Arizona senator, former P.O.W. and presidential candidate. His spokesman read a letter written by McCain, his own Farewell Address, in which he said:[94]

Fellow Americans, that association has meant more to me than any other. I lived and died a proud American. We are citizens of the world's greatest republic. A nation of ideals, not blood and soil. We are blessed and a blessing to humanity when we uphold and advance those ideals at home and in the world. We have helped liberate more people from tyranny and poverty than ever before in history.

You should read the entirety of the senator's final statement for yourself. I cannot do it without crying. This passage is again a declaration of the power of the people. And the American people have greater power than those of any nation in history. We have cast off the chains of kings and of slaves. We have beaten back oppression, genocide, and autocracy, and kept it at bay on the world's doorstep for decades. We have split the atom and reached

---

93 Susan B. Glasser, "John McCain's Funeral Was the Biggest Resistance Meeting Yet," *The New Yorker*, September 1, 2018. https://www.newyorker.com/news/letter-from-trumps-washington/john-mccains-funeral-was-the-biggest-resistance-meeting-yet

94 John Sidney McCain III, farewell statement ready by Rick Davis at the Washington National Cathedral, September 1, 2018. https://www.politico.com/story/2018/08/27/full-text-john-mccains-farewell-statement-797487

the moon. We have laid rails and roadways across a continent and forged a vast, new world out of the tiniest electrons. The power of the people can do great things, terrible things, and sometimes both at once. That is the riddle of steel—those who unite the people hold the power.

Steel is, of course, representative of all of technology. Steve Jobs, co-founder of the Apple Computer Company, was another American icon who understood the riddle of steel. In a 1994 interview with *Rolling Stone* magazine, he said:[95]

> *Technology is nothing. What's important is that you have faith in people, that they're basically good and smart, and if you give them tools, they'll do wonderful things with them. It's not the tools that you have faith in — tools are just tools. They work, or they don't work. It's people you have faith in or not.*

Faith in people means defending their freedom and liberty. The only government that can deliver on the defense of these foundational rights is a robust democracy coupled to a free market. People must be free to strive, free to live, free to love, and free to fail. The government must set guardrails to protect the greater good, but must always remember that the power is with the people. As American

---

[95] Marcel Schwantes, "Steve Jobs: 'Technology is nothing'—here's what he said it really takes to achieve great success," *CNBC*, October 5, 2019, 9:15 AM EDT.
https://www.cnbc.com/2019/10/05/apple-ceo-steve-jobs-technology-is-nothing-heres-what-it-takes-to-achieve-great-success.html

centrists, we must remind our leaders and our citizens of that by speaking out, by writing to our representatives, sometimes by walking the streets, and always by voting. When we are too busy to go to the polls or won't take the time to communicate with our elected officials, then liberty dies just a little bit. We forget the price that we must pay for freedom at our own peril.

The Prayer of the Centrist

It was November of 2024, and I had just voted in the most divisive and perhaps most consequential election of my life. The talk in the voting line itself revealed just how divided the country had become. It was all about Trump, of course. The Democrats had worked hard to convince voters that democracy itself was at stake in the election, and there were people in line whose banter clarified that they absolutely believed this to be the case. The Republicans had worked hard to paint Kamala Harris as an elite insider and Trump as the only one thinking about working families and capable of draining the swamp. There were enough red caps in the line to proclaim broad support for this perspective also.

I was also thinking ahead to Thanksgiving, when we were to have a houseful of visiting family, bringing with them a spectrum of views on politics and on religion. We would have my father-in-law, a traditional conservative whose remarkable career had included roles as chief of staff and campaign manager to U.S. Representatives and was a Republican state legislator himself. We would have my own gender-nonconforming kid, a self-described atheistic ceramic artist sporting a growing number of tattoos. We would have stockbrokers and scientists, bankers and bakers. What would we talk about? Would it remain respectful? Would we say grace before the holiday meal? I sat down to write, and I provide the following attempt at a unifying message for your consideration.

The Prayer of the Centrist

O God of so many inscrutable aspects,
if you are all things, then you must be
the source both of violence and of beauty in the world,
held in constant tension within our human instincts.

You are named by some as Jesus or as Brahman,
and by others as Allah, Yahweh, or Gitche Manitou.

To some, you are the earth or the sky.

To others, you are the ceaseless flow of the Tao
through all of space and time.

To others still, you are simply Nature...or Fortune.

But for those of us here who believe in Truth,
and in spirituality in any of its forms,
from faith, to art, to mathematics,
for those of us whose intuition tells us that there is some mystery,
hidden within the Universe,
that connects all things,
and for those of us who feel the struggle for balance
between life and death in the world all around us,
we offer this benediction.

May those whom we love be safe and healthy.

May we each experience the satisfaction of meeting our personal goals,
and in helping others to achieve their own.

May we all see that we are connected to our neighbors,
as well as to the greater body of human culture and civilization.

May our thoughts and actions be guided by a selfless desire
to advance the greater good.

Amen.

My fears were completely unfounded. I am lucky in that, on both my wife's side and my side of the family, love for each other prevails. There were no awkward questions, no challenges offered, no offense taken. We were all just happy to see each other and to spend time together. The printed paper with the Prayer of the Centrist upon it stayed planted in my pocket.

Reflecting on it now, after gradually working out this manifesto over the last year, I have to say that the prayer is just too passive. Someone said once that God helps those who help themselves. Wishing our problems away is not going to do it. We need to be actively engaged.

My father-in-law and I absolutely see eye-to-eye on many things. The importance of family, service to the Nation, working hard and doing your best, to name a few. I would also say that we respect each other as we see each other's strengths. He knows me well and gave me a book that he thought I might find interesting, *The Fourth Turning is Here*, by Neil Howe.[96]

This work discusses the cycles of history whose period is that of a long human lifetime, roughly a century. As the Earth itself goes through seasons, so are there seasons of human society. The summer of civilization is a great awakening where the people cast off the bonds of convention to recreate our internal values. This was the 1960s and the era of civil rights and free love. Winter is a

---

[96] Neil Howe, *The Fourth Turning is Here*, Simon & Schuster, New York (2023).

time of crisis, often broad and cataclysmic conflict, when the architecture of civilization is tested and then crumbles. Last experienced in World War II, our governments, treaties, and externally facing values must then be rebuilt as the crisis winds down. The length of each cycle is just long enough for the people to begin to forget the hardships and horrors of the last crisis. How many World War II veterans do we have remaining amongst the living today?

Indeed, Howe proposes that we are now living within a new time of crisis, and the world order will again change in the next decade. And so history repeats itself, with each generation trapped according to its phase within the cycle, locked into a predictable psyche and fated to experience the predestined pattern of history.

It may seem to you that history is linear, with the technological aptitude of our species and our quality of life only increasing in time, but this is because you are sampling a very local region where you happen to sit on a great, spinning wheel. In Howe's view, a crash is coming.

His chapter on *The Millenial Crisis* is downright terrifying. Howe tracks the progressing partisan division that we have seen in our country since the turn of the millenium, all but predicting the government shutdown in 2025. He concludes that we are likely to see civil war, great-power conflict, or both within the next decade. Like I said— terrifying. The invasion of Ukraine by Russia could be the start of a building global war. The American population, with geographically intermixed leftists and right-wingers, is like a cocktail of fuel and oxygen just waiting for a spark.

111

We sit on a powder keg within a house of dynamite,[97] and we'll ignite an implosion from within unless an explosion detonates around us first.

One sees the patterns of cyclical behavior all through history, but Timothy Snyder provides a counterpoint. I found his book *On Tyranny* at a game store in Spokane, oddly displayed right next to the cash register, as if to say, "Would you like an historically rigorous and politically astute treatise on autocracy with your Dungeon Master's Guide?" Well, I guess it worked—I picked up a copy.

Snyder explains that linear and cyclical thinking about history can both be mental traps that inhibit us from taking any meaningful action in the political sphere:[98]

> *If you once did nothing because you thought progress is inevitable, then you can continue to do nothing because you think time moves in repeating cycles.*

Snyder also never mentions Trump's name but clearly intends to suggest lessons for today. Trumpism itself is perhaps just a symptom, a manifestation of our season of winter within the cycle. If it had not been Trump, then it would have been someone else donning the mantle of populism in our time. But I agree with Snyder's statement.

---

[97] *A House of Dynamite*, directed by Kathryn Bigelow, written by Noah Oppenheim, Netflix (2025).
https://www.imdb.com/title/tt32376165/

[98] Timothy Snyder, *On Tyranny: Twenty Lessons from the Twentieth Century,* Tim Duggan Books, New York (2017).

We do not have to accept that we are victims of history. We are always present in a moment that is unique in its own way. We can listen to the echoes of history as a guide, but the future will respond to the effort that we put into creating it. American centrism can lay before us a gentler path, dampen the swing of the pendulum, or itself could be the change in perception and action that resolves Howe's time of crisis and moves the wheel forward into its next phase. A renewed focus on centrism could be the key to defuse or at least to dampen our internal civil strife, and a unified, reinvigorated American spirit would deter the aggressive march of autocracy in the world.

So, why did I write this manifesto? I mean, I'm nobody, and who knows if anyone will read this. My wife is convinced that this manifesto is basically a big personal therapy session, and maybe she's right. But I also wrote it with a purpose in mind. I wrote it because it feels like we need a new forcing function in the world. One that points to the center and to democracy, rather than middle America being held in a brutal tension by forces on the *left* and on the *right*. And we need people willing to take action, to defend the center with passionate intensity. Maybe if I have the courage to articulate this message, someone will hear it, elaborate on it, and pass it on. If two people do that, then another two, then two more…it will catch fire. Maybe. Or maybe no one will read it. I guess we'll see.

It can feel like the political center has no control, stranded in a rudderless raft in the midst of a vast ocean, victim of the tides. But we have to remember that the independents actually run the show. Or at least we should. We are the targets of all the political ads—they seek our favor and our contested votes. We are the ones who tip the scales in elections. We should do this deliberately, with American centrism as the lever arm. We need to convince politicians to embrace centrism and to work across the aisle. We need all voters to reject candidates who are blatantly partisan and who represent political factions seeking power rather than the greater good.

We need to remember that America is not a place, it's a people. Yes, I am quoting a Marvel movie,[99] but think about it. America is you and your family. It's your babies, smiling at you for the first time. It's your neighbors. It's your relatives at Thanksgiving. It's not a bunch of abstract red states and blue states. It is certainly not a collection of wealthy, elite politicians and tech billionaires. It's a bunch of, well, nobodies. As Cunningham says (Lehigh-Valley Don Cunningham, this time), it is *us*. It is *We the People*. And it is about time that *We the People* started demanding that government and politicians listen to voices in the middle, find a way to compromise on policy issues, and make ethical, nonpartisan administrative decisions so that government can be effective. We must demand that politicians turn their focus away from power for its own sake and toward the good of the Nation.

I'll leave you with one final thought. You have to take the initiative to get things done in life. You need to use your

---

[99] *Thor: Ragnarok*, directed by Taika Waititi, written by Eric Pearson, Craig Kyle, and Christopher L. Yost, Marvel Studios (2017). https://www.imdb.com/title/tt3501632/quotes/

common sense and figure it out. You can't blame anyone else—it's up to you to do it, and you might have to keep your hand in the box for a minute here. You need to take the political system by the horns. Write to your state and federal representatives in Congress. Volunteer for a political campaign to support a centrist candidate in a tough primary. Talk about centrist politics with your family and your neighbors. Take to the streets and scream, "BE REASONABLE!" And then vote!

> *...policies don't change until the public ethic changes. Like, even...even when things get to the Supreme Court, for example, when big changes happen in the courts, they kind of need a public push. That's what we saw with the Civil Rights decisions of the Supreme Court. It's what we saw with gay marriage. It's sort of like, when things need to happen in the culture first, and then you see them happen in the agencies. You see pressure on politicians. You even see pressure on courts. So I do think that it starts with us...it starts with people, and it trickles up. I'm really convinced of that.*

— Cynthia Barnett[100]

---

[100] Laura Paskus and Andy Lyman, "Episode 11: A reverence for rivers," *Lesser Known New Mexico Podcast*, September 30, 2025. https://lesserknownnmpod.substack.com/p/episode-11-a-reverence-for-rivers

Appendix: Write to Congress

You may copy this text using the QR code at the end of this book. It is not hard to contact your state and federal representatives!

https://www.congress.gov/members/find-your-member

Dear _____,

I believe in the rule of law rooted in the Constitution, in government for the people, in treating others with respect, and in evidence-based decision making.

I support the platform of the American centrist:

Uphold voting rights—ensure all citizens have access to the polls and voting is made easy with options such as early voting and mail-in ballots.

Abolish gerrymandering—mandate independent redistricting commissions. I will not vote for you if you participate in partisan or retributive redistricting.

Require open primaries—all elections supported with public funds must allow all voters to participate.

Poisonous partisan polarization must stop. You must compromise and move toward the center if you want to earn the votes of America's passionate moderates.

Sincerely, _____

Let your representatives know how you feel about political issues! If they see a centrist path, they will move there. Here's what I will say.

Dear _____,

It is time to end the polarized politics that are driving people apart in our nation. I am an independent voter and a moderate centrist. I demand that you work across the aisle and be willing to compromise.

I support the following reasonable steps to resolve recurring wedge issues that have paralyzed America:

- Federal guarantee for full abortion rights before 24 weeks of pregnancy, with states deciding after that.

- Strong universal background checks before all gun ownership, age requirement of 21, red flag laws, and holding owners accountable for securing firearms, while retaining the legal right to own assault weapons.

- Protect and respect our minority populations. Halt the wave of animosity toward transgender people, uphold the Respect for Marriage Act, and ensure that minorities can vote in every election.

Proactive leadership is required from our representatives to stabilize national policy on these issues and allow our energy to be focused on key topics such as the economy, national security, and defense of democracy in the world. I will vote for candidates who commit to centrism in this.

Sincerely, _____

Or, you might just be pissed off. Your representatives in the state and federal government need to hear that. Here's how I would do it.

Dear _____,

It is time to end the polarized politics that are hurting the people of our nation. I am an independent voter and an American centrist. I demand that you do the work to compromise and make government effective.

Congress has not passed a full budget on time since 1997. The patchwork of Continuing Resolutions and government shutdowns are hurting the effectiveness of federal workers and contractors by causing endless replanning and sub-optimal deployment of funds to hedge for uncertainty. This affects programs supporting national security and degrades U.S. capability and strategic objectives. Passing a budget on time is your core job. Do your job. You must negotiate across the aisle well in advance of votes on budget bills and ensure that funding of federal priorities is stable and predictable.

You need to take responsibility for building relationships across all parties so that America can get things done. I am sick and tired of how things are going in our country. We need to turn it around. If you cannot demonstrate that you can move to the center, compromise, pass reasonable legislation, and make our government work, then you will lose my vote. I look forward to transparent and frequent communication from you on your progress.

Sincerely, _____

Do you want your teenager to read this book in order to facilitate a discussion on politics and morality, but you can't get their attention away from screens? Show them this page, then ask them to review the *Moderate Manifesto* and determine how this is relevant. If you get a reasonable explanation, then please let me know what you learn, too.

I showed this page to my kids. They smirked and said, "Dad, this will be out of date before you publish it." That may be true, but nothing lasts forever. How ephemeral is democracy? Barbarism or autocracy may return, unless we are willing to do the work as advocates for centrism.

More information on *The American Centrist*, draft letters to Congress, and a link to order this book in print are here: